The Victims of "Dick and Jane" and Other Essays

Other Books
by Samuel L. Blumenfeld

How to Start Your Own Private School and Why You Need One

The New Illiterates

The Retreat from Motherhood

How to Tutor

Alpha-Phonics: A Primer for Beginning Readers

Is Public Education Necessary?

NEA: Trojan Horse in American Education

The Whole Language/OBE Fraud

Homeschooling: A Parents' Guide to Teaching Children

The Victims of "Dick and Jane"

and Other Essays

Samuel L. Blumenfeld

Chalcedon
Vallecito, California
2003

Address all inquiries to:

Chalcedon
P. O. Box 158
Vallecito, CA 95251
U.S.A.

Library of Congress Cataloging-in-Publication Data

Blumenfeld, Samuel L.
The Victims of "Dick and Jane" and Other Essays
Samuel L. Blumenfeld
Includes index
ISBN 1-891375-21-0

Printed in the United States of America

First Edition

Dedicated to

The Blessed Memory of

Reverend Rousas J. Rushdoony

(1916 - 2001)

Contents

Preface

The essays in this book were written over a period of time from the 1980s to the present and were originally published in a number of different periodicals, including my own newsletter which is no longer being published. Most of them are on the subject of education, and therefore the reader will find recurrent themes in the different essays. I often found it necessary to repeat important facts in different essays because I wanted as many readers as possible to become aware of these facts. Thus, I hope the reader will forgive me if he finds the repetition annoying.

I became interested in education, and particularly in the teaching of reading, when a lawyer friend of mine by the name of Watson Washburn came to my office at Grosset & Dunlap, where, in 1963, I was an editor, and asked me to become a member of his Advisory Council. He had just created the Reading Reform Foundation because of his concern with the reading problem. His aim, he said, was to get phonics back in the schools. This surprised me. Since when had phonics been removed, I asked. How could you possibly teach reading without it? The first essay in this book explains the rest of the story.

In 1970 I decided to start writing books full-time. I approached my publisher friend, the late Neil McCaffrey, founder of the Conservative Book Club, with some book ideas. He wanted a book on how to start a private school and asked if I could write one.

There was at the time a burgeoning alternative education movement. I did some preliminary research and decided that I could do such a book. And so I wrote, *How to Start Your Own Private School and Why You Need One.*

The research for that book led me into the labyrinth of America's education system and its reading problem. So in my second book, *The New Illiterates,* I tried to find out why the reading problem persisted in 1970 after Rudolf Flesch had revealed the cause of the problem in 1955. Of course, the cause was the fundamental change in reading instruction from phonics to look-say. In fact, just about everything in primary education had been changed. Penmanship had been discarded in favor of print script, and the New Math had destroyed simple arithmetic.

And so, in 1973 I decided that, since the educators were not going to get back to the kind of basics that parents wanted, it was necessary to give parents the tools to do the teaching of the basic academic skills at home. The result was *How to Tutor.* Out of that book came *Alpha-Phonics: A Primer for Beginning Readers*, which has been successfully used by thousands of homeschoolers in America and abroad to teach their children to read in the proper phonetic way.

Naturally, in writing about public education one must deal with educational philosophy. This led me to ask two questions: (1) What was behind the change in educational philosophy that had so radically altered the curriculum in the public schools? And (2) why did Americans give up educational freedom so early in their history for a government system that virtually took total responsibility for the education of children? To get the answers, I embarked on a research project, assisted by a grant from the Institute for Humane Studies, which finally resulted in my book, *Is Public Education Necessary?*

The four years of research for that book opened my eyes to how government education had been foisted on the American people by the Harvard Unitarians, Owenite Socialists, Hegelians, and liberal Protestants. The only people who opposed it were the orthodox Calvinists who understood the long-range problems that secular, government-owned and -controlled education would create. And today, we see the full flower of moral corruption that secular public education has inevitably brought about.

And so, I have had much to write about in cataloging the horrors of the education system we are saddled with. In 1984 I wrote *NEA: Trojan Horse in American Education,* because I wanted the American public to know the depth and strength of the political power that the organized educators were able to wield over America. Because public education was government owned, it was subject to political manipulation by whomever had the power to do the manipulating. And it wasn't the parents who dutifully sent their children to these schools. It was the educators who had learned how to manipulate legislators in order to get what they wanted at the expense of the taxpayer.

But nothing remains the same for very long in America. And so I have chronicled the changes taking place: the growth of the homeschool movement, the Christian revival, the further deterioration of American literacy. I hope the reader will enjoy and gain from what I have written. Meanwhile, I wish to thank Chalcedon for bringing out these essays in book form so that their message could be diffused far and wide to the benefit of our blessed country and its people.

Samuel L. Blumenfeld
Waltham, Massachusetts
October, 2002

The Victims of "Dick and Jane"

A National Blight

"Illiteracy in this country is turning out to be a blight that won't go away." So stated John H. Sweet, chairman of *U. S. News & World Report*, in his introduction to the magazine's cover story of May 17, 1982, on America's declining literacy. He further observed: "While the United States has the highest proportion of its young people in college of any major nation, it has not yet figured out how to teach tens of millions of its citizens to fill out a job application, balance a checkbook, read a newspaper or write a simple letter."

Illiteracy has now joined unwed motherhood, herpes simplex, and budget deficits as one of the nation's insoluble problems that get periodic attention in the media with the usual call that something be done about it. Americans, however, are already paying an army of over two million teachers who supposedly *are* doing something about it. They are the experts and professionals, with college degrees and certification. We have a universal compulsory education system that costs taxpayers over $100 billion a year, created to guarantee that everyone in America learns to read and write. So we have teachers, we have schools, we have laws. We have more educational research than we know what to do with. But the system evidently doesn't work.

In fact, among people who have had as much as twelve years of schooling, there is an ever-growing population of functional illiterates — people who cannot read training manuals, books, magazines, or product labels written above a fourth or fifth-grade level. Some parents have gone so far as to sue public school systems for graduating their children without teaching them adequate literacy skills so that they can get jobs. Experts' estimates of the extent of functional illiteracy among our adult population range from twenty-five to fifty percent. It may account for the decline in voter turnout and the growing dependence on television as the sole source of information and knowledge.

According to Vyvyan Harding, director of Literacy Services of Wisconsin, which provides reading tutors to functionally illiterate adults, "It seems like a futile battle against overwhelming odds. I've never seen so many non-reading adults in my life."

Nor is this decline in literacy skills limited to the lower-income, less academically inclined population. Karl Shapiro, the eminent poet-professor who has taught creative writing for more than twenty years, told the California Library Association in 1970: "What is really distressing is that this generation cannot and does not read. I am speaking of university students in what are supposed to be our best universities. Their illiteracy is staggering.... We are experiencing a literacy breakdown which is unlike anything I know of in the history of letters."

Literacy skills are now so poor among high school graduates that about two-thirds of U.S. colleges and universities, including Harvard, MIT, and the University of California at Berkeley, provide remedial reading and writing courses for their freshmen. The decline in reading skills is also causing a general debasement of our use of language. Popular writers, seeking larger audiences among a shrinking number of readers are using shorter sentences, more monosyllabic words, and much smaller, simpler vocabularies. Complex ideas are very often avoided because the vocabulary required to deal with them is too difficult for most readers. So we get high school and college textbooks that treat the complexities of life with comic book simplicity and novels written without richness of language or depth of character. To many Americans, highly literate English is now a foreign language.

All of which may lead any intelligent American to ask a number of pointed questions: Why should the world's most affluent and advanced nation, with free *compulsory* education for all, have a "reading problem" in the first place? What, indeed, are the kids doing in school if not learning to read? How is it that our network of state-owned and -operated teachers colleges with strict certification requirements doesn't produce teachers who can teach?

And how is it that in a nation that has devoted more of its money and resources to education than any other nation in history, we find a Jonathan Kozol on the *MacNeil-Leher Report* advocating that we learn from Communist Cuba how to eradicate illiteracy in America? Is our much-vaunted educational system indeed inferior to that of Castro's Cuba? How is it that our educators are in a quandary over our declining literacy skills and don't know what to do about it except ask for more money? And how is it that the more federal money is poured into public education the worse the SAT scores get?

Don't expect any answers to come from the people in charge. If they knew the answers, we would not have the problem. But the answers do exist, and the reason why they have gotten very little attention in the media is that they are too incredible, and our educators will neither confirm nor deny them. The result is that the public doesn't know who or what to believe.

Why Johnny Can't Read

The trouble is that you have to become an expert if you want to confront the educators on their own turf. My own introduction to the reading problem began in 1962 when Watson Washburn, who had just founded the Reading Reform Foundation, asked me to become a member of his national advisory council. Washburn, a distinguished New York attorney, had become concerned about the reading problem when he discovered that several of his nieces and nephews, who were attending the city's finest private schools, were having a terrible time learning to read. He found that they were being taught to read via the "look-say" method, a method that Rudolf Flesch had exposed and denounced in his 1955 book, *Why Johnny Can't Read.*

Flesch had written the book to explain to a somewhat baffled public why more and more primary-school children were having enormous difficulties learning to read, difficulties that parents had already begun to notice and complain about in the 1940s. The incisive, Vienna-born author was quite blunt in identifying the cause of the problem: "The teaching of reading all over the United States, in all the schools, and in all the textbooks," he wrote, "is totally wrong and flies in the face of all logic and common sense." He then went on to explain that from about 1930 to 1950, beginning reading instruction in American schools had been radically changed by the professors of education from the traditional alphabetic-phonics method to a new whole-word, or hieroglyphic, method. Written English was no longer taught as a sound-symbol system but as an ideographic system, like Chinese. This was news to a lot of parents who assumed that their children were being taught to read the way they had been taught. How else could you possibly learn to read? they wondered.

In 1962, despite Flesch, the schools were still teaching the look-say method, which is why Washburn created the Reading Reform Foundation — to try to get the alphabet and phonics back into primary education as the dominant form of reading instruction. At that time, I was a book editor in New York and had little interest in primary education.

But the foundation's goal seemed quite laudable, so I joined the advisory council.

That was the extent of my involvement with the reading problem until I started working on my first book, *How to Start Your Own Private School — And Why You Need One*. In researching that book, I had spent eighteen months of 1970-71 substitute teaching in the public schools of Quincy, Massachusetts, in order to get a first-hand view of what was going on in the American classroom. I suddenly became aware that a great many high school students were reading very poorly. In fact, some of the students reminded me of the foreign-born I had grown up with in New York. They read in that same halting, stumbling manner.

My parents, immigrants from Eastern Europe, had both been illiterate in English. My mother had no literacy in any language even though she was quite intelligent; she was simply the product of Old World poverty and neglect. Her children, however — three of whom were born in Europe; two, including myself, in the United States — all learned to read and write quite fluently in the public schools of New York with no apparent problems. Although no one ever spoke of the alphabet as a "sound-symbol system," we were all aware that the alphabet letters stood for sounds.

Yet I remember the terrible difficulty I had when I tried to teach my mother to read. Her illiteracy had been something of a challenge to me. It seemed like such an appalling state for a normally intelligent person to be in: to have no access at all to the world of the written word; not to be able to read street signs, advertisements, newspapers, magazines. Thus, I grew up very much aware of the terrible limitations illiteracy placed on a person and also of the frustrations and shame it sometimes caused. My mother tried going to night school, but the teachers were unprepared for total illiteracy, and my mother returned home humiliated by the experience.

And so, while going to City College, I decided to try to teach my mother to read. I started off by teaching her the alphabet. She learned it quite well. But then I was not too sure how to proceed from there. So I started teaching her to read whole words in short sentences, like: *Sara is my name. My name is Sara.* She learned to repeat the sentences, but she did not learn to read them. I didn't know what was wrong. I tried to convey the idea that letters stood for sounds, but I did it rather haphazardly, as an afterthought, as if the idea was so obvious that anyone could catch on to it. It's so simple, I thought impatiently, why can't she learn it?

What I didn't realize is that an illiterate, as well as a small child, has no conception of a set of written symbols standing for the irreducible speech sounds of a language. The assumption of the illiterate is that printed words represent ideas rather than sounds. To an illiterate who does not have a key to the sound-symbol code, printed words are therefore undecipherable markings.

What I also didn't realize is that our alphabet system is somewhat complicated. We use twenty-six letters to represent forty-four sounds; there is an important distinction to be made between the letter names and letter sounds. And because the system has many quaint irregularities, it has to be taught in a logical, organized sequence, starting with the simplest regular combinations and proceeding to the more complex irregular ones.

Had I known this, I would have known how to teach my mother to read. Unfortunately, my own ignorance was so appalling that I gave up in the attempt and blamed my failure on my mother's inability to learn. It took me twenty-five years to find out what an ignoramus I had been. In the meantime, my mother had died and the problem of teaching reading in America had become the educational dilemma of the century.

When my book on private schools was completed, I suggested to my publisher that I do one on the reading problem. My confrontation with the semiliterates in the schools of Quincy had opened my eyes to its seriousness, and I was curious to find out why, fifteen years after the publication of *Why Johnny Can't Read*, Johnny was still fumbling and mumbling the written word. My publisher liked the idea, and I got to work.

The Roots of the Look-Say Method

First, I wanted to find out what it was about the look-say, whole-word method that made it the cause of so much reading disability. So I decided to study one of the whole-word programs, going through the entire "Dick and Jane" course of instruction, page-by-page, line by line, from the pre-readers to the third-grade readers. It was an excruciating, tedious task, and the more I read, the angrier I got. I could not understand how professors of education could have concocted an approach to reading instruction so needlessly complicated, difficult, illogical, and ineffective. This look-say method was far worse than Flesch had described it in his book. You had to be an expert guesser or have a photographic memory to get anywhere with it. I knew that if I had been subjected to this blatant educational malpractice at the age of six, I too would likely have wound up among the reading disabled.

But how was it possible for such an imbecilic method to have come to use so universally in American primary schools? I became determined to find out who had started it all. What "educator" was insane enough to think that you could successfully teach children to read English as if it were Chinese? After considerable digging through the historical archives, I found the "culprit." But he turned out not to be a culprit at all. In fact, he turned out to be someone quite interesting, important, and sympathetic.

He was Thomas H. Galladuet, the venerable founder of the Hartford Asylum for the Deaf and Dumb. I discovered that his *Mother's Primer*, first published in 1835, was the first look-say primer to appear. I had the pleasure of inspecting a rare copy of the book, which is kept in a vault at Gallaudet College in Washington, D. C. Its first line reads: "Frank had a dog; his name was Spot."

Gallaudet was an unusual teacher who brought to the learning problems of the deaf and dumb great empathy and a talent for innovation. He thought he could apply to normal children some of the techniques used to teach deaf-mutes to read. Since deaf-mutes have no conception of a spoken language, they could not learn a sound-symbol system of reading. Instead, they were taught to read by way of a purely sight method consisting of pictures and whole words. Thus, as far as the deaf pupil was concerned, the written language represented ideas only and had nothing to do with sounds made by the tongue and vocal chords. Might not such a method work even better with normal children?

In 1836, the Boston Primary School Committee decided to try Gallaudet's primer on an experimental basis. Horace Mann, who became secretary of the Massachusetts Board of Education in June 1837, was very critical of the traditional alphabetic teaching method, and he heartily endorsed the new method as a means of liberating children from academic tyranny. In November the Primary School Committee reported favorably on the Gallaudet primer, and it was officially adopted for use in the Boston primary schools. Pretty soon other textbook writers got on the whole-word bandwagon and they began producing their own versions of the Gallaudet primer.

All of this took place in the context of a great movement for universal public education, which was expected to eradicate the ills of mankind by applying science and rationality to education. In 1839 Mann and his fellow reformers established the first state-owned and -operated college for teacher training — the Normal School at Lexington, Massachusetts. Gallaudet had been offered the school's directorship but declined it. The man who did accept the post, Cyrus W. Peirce, was just as enthusiastic about the whole-word method as Mann. And so, in the very first year of the very first state teachers college in America, the whole-word method of reading instruction was taught to its students as the preferred and superior method of instruction. Thus, educational quackery not only got a great running start with state-controlled teacher training but became a permanent part of it.

During the next five years, Mann's *Common School Journal* became the propaganda medium not only of the public school movement and the state normal schools but of its quackery — particularly the whole-word method. But finally, in 1844, there was an incredible reaction. A group of Boston schoolmasters, who had had enough of the nonsense, published a blistering book-length attack on Mann and his reforms. Included in the attack was a thorough, detailed, and incisive critique of the whole-word method, the first such critique ever to be written.

This attack ignited a bitter dispute between Mann and the schoolmasters that was to last for more than a year and result in a return to common sense in primary reading instruction. The state normal schools, fledgling institutions at best, were simply not yet powerful enough to exert a decisive influence in the local classroom. Professors of education were still a long way off in the future. So the alphabetic method was restored to its proper place in primary instruction. But the whole-word method was kept alive in the normal schools as a legitimate alternative until it could be refurbished by a new generation of reformers in the new progressive age.

The Influence of John Dewey

The whole-word method began to make its comeback around the turn of the century and eventually took over modern primary instruction. A new progressive philosophy of education was being propounded by socialist John Dewey, who wanted to change the focus of education from the development of individual academic skills to the development of cooperative social skills. The object of socialism had been from the very beginning to remake man from the competitive being of capitalist society to a cooperative being in a collectivist state. Education was considered the best means to achieve this. Dewey's famous Laboratory School at the University of Chicago (1896-1904) and later, the Lincoln School (1917-46) at Teachers College, Columbia University, where Dewey opened shop in 1905, set the new direction for teacher education.

Curiously enough, one of the patrons of the Lincoln School was John D. Rockefeller, Jr., who sent four of his five sons to be educated there. Jules Abel, in his book on the Rockefellers, revealed some interesting details about what the Lincoln School did for the boys' literacy:

> The influence of the Lincoln School, which as a progressive school, encouraged students to explore their own interests and taught them to live in society has been a dominant one in their lives.... Yet Laurance gives startling confirmation as to "Why Johnnie Can't Read." He says that the Lincoln School did not teach him to read and write as he wishes he now could. Nelson, today, admits that reading for him is a "slow

> and tortuous process" that he does not enjoy doing but compels himself to do it. This is significant evidence in the debate that has raged about modern educational techniques.

The tragedy is that there are millions of Americans like the Rockefellers who must endure the crippling consequences of such malpractice.

It is, of course, no accident that the two leading developers and advocates of the new teaching method spent their entire careers at the two main centers where John Dewey's influence was greatest and where most of the progressive ferment was taking place. William Scott Gray joined the faculty at the University of Chicago in 1914 and was dean of its college of education from 1917 to 1931. He was chief editor of the Scott S. Foresman & Co. "Dick and Jane" basal reading program from 1930 until his death in 1960.

Arthur I. Gates toiled in the vineyards of Columbia Teachers College as a professor of education from 1917 to 1965. He was chief editor of the publisher Macmillan's basal reading program from 1930 well into the 60s. He died in 1972.

Both Gray and Gates wrote hundreds of articles on reading instruction for the professional journals as well as numerous textbooks used in teacher training. Gray was especially instrumental in organizing the International Reading Association in 1955. It has become the world's largest and most influential professional organization devoted to reading instruction, and it is perhaps the only organization of such size in which a form of educational malpractice has been enshrined as the highest pedagogical good and its practitioners awarded prizes for their "achievements."

While Flesch was the first to expose look-say to the general public, he was not the first to question the new method's soundness or to confront the professors with its potentially harmful effects. The first to do that was Dr. Samuel T. Orton, a neuropathologist, who in 1929 published an article in *Educational Psychology* reporting that many children could not learn to read via the new whole-word method. He warned that this method "may not only prevent the acquisition of academic education by children of average capacity but may also give rise to far-reaching damage to their emotional life."

Orton had discovered all of this in the 1920s while investigating cases of reading disability in Iowa, where the new method was being widely used. But the professors of education decided that Orton didn't know much about education and went ahead with their plans to publish the new basal reading programs. Later they made use of Orton's own medical diagnoses and terminology to identify what was wrong with the kids having trouble learning to read. But they never admitted that it was the teaching method that caused these problems to develop.

So, as early as 1929, the educators had had some warning from a prominent physician that the new whole-word method could cause serious reading disability. Despite this, the new basal reading programs turned out to be huge commercial successes as whole school districts switched over to Dick and Jane, Alice and Jerry, Janet and Mark, Jimmy and Sue, Tom and Betty, and other whole-word basal series that were earning substantial royalties for their professor-of-education authors.

The Educational Monopoly

By the 1940s, schools everywhere were setting up remedial reading departments and reading clinics to handle the thousands of children with reading problems. In fact, remedial teaching had blossomed into a whole new educational specialty with its own professional status, and educational research on reading problems had become a new growth industry.

Researchers, seeking the causes of growing reading disability, began to develop a whole new lexicon of exotic terms to deal with this previously unknown problem: congenital word blindness, word deafness, developmental alexia, congenital alexia, congenital aphasia, dyslexia, strephosymbolia, binocular imbalance, ocular blocks, dyslexaphoria, ocular-manual laterality, minimal brain damage, and whatever else sounded plausible.

What were the cures recommended for these horrible diseases? *Life* magazine, in a major article on dyslexia in 1944, described the cure recommended by the Dyslexia Institute at Northwestern University for one little girl with an I.Q. of 118: thyroid treatments, removal of tonsils and adenoids, exercises to strengthen her eye muscles. It's a wonder they didn't suggest a prefrontal lobotomy. With the boom in remedial teaching also came the creation of professional organizations to deal with it. In 1946 the National Association for Remedial Teaching was founded, and two years later the International Council for the Improvement of Reading Instruction was organized. Both organizations held annual conventions, published bulletins, and provided publishers the opportunity to exhibit their wares.

At this point, one might ask, how could the professors get away with this blatant educational malpractice in a free country where parents and elected representatives are supposed to have ultimate control over the public schools? Flesch gave the answer:

> It's a foolproof system all right. Every grade-school teacher in the country has to go to a teachers' college or school of education; every teachers' college gives at least one course on how to teach reading; every course on how to teach reading is based on a textbook; every one of those textbooks is written by one of the high priests of the word method. In the old days it was impossible to keep a good teacher from following her own common sense and practical knowledge; today the phonetic system of teaching reading is kept out of our schools as effectively as if we had a dictatorship with an all-powerful Ministry of Education.

Apparently, government-monopolized education, even without a dictatorship, is quite capable of stifling dissent. In the matter of reading instruction, what we have had to contend with is a private monopoly of professors of education within a state-controlled and regulated system. These professors had a strong economic and professional interest in pushing and keeping their textbooks and methodology in the schools, and the state system made it easy for them to create a monopoly and maintain it indefinitely. Teacher certification laws require that young teachers be trained by these educators, who not only prepare the curriculum for teacher training but also hold sway over the professional journals the teachers read and the organizations they join. In addition, the professors of education are organized professionally along national lines and therefore can exert a nationwide influence over the teaching profession as a whole.

As state institutions, the public schools are well protected from the forces that normally determine the success or failure of a private enterprise. Monopolies flourish in the public sector because of the latter's hierarchical, bureaucratic structure, which rewards conformity and discourages competition. Those who work their way up to positions of power and control in the hierarchy use that power by way of tenure to solidify and perpetuate their control. They supervise the doctoral programs and set the standards for promotion within the hierarchy, and they advance only those who support them. Thus, the system is self-perpetuating.

The Educational Establishment Counterattacks

What was the reaction of the professors of education to the publication in 1955 of *Why Johnny Can't Read*? They denounced Flesch in no uncertain terms, accusing him of misrepresentation, oversimplification, and superficiality. Arthur Gates wrote an article in the *National Education Association Journal* entitled "Why Mr. Flesch is Wrong," which the textbook publisher Macmillan reprinted for wider distribution among parents and teachers. Other authors of whole-word classroom materials referred to Horace Mann's endorsement of the method. Of course, they never pointed out that Mann was a lawyer, not an educator, and that he never taught primary school.

William S. Gray, to whom the profession looked for leadership, did an article for the *Reading Teacher* of December 1955 entitled "Phonic versus Other Methods of Teaching Reading." In the same issue, F. Duane Lamkin of the University of Virginia wrote a piece entitled "An Analysis of Propaganda Techniques Used in *Why Johnny Can't Read.*"

To Gray, the Flesch attack was actually nothing new. In 1951 there had been so much lay criticism of whole-word reading instruction that the *Reading Teacher* of May 15, 1952, published an article entitled "How Can We Meet the Attacks?" In the January 1952 issue of *Progressive Education*, Gray had specifically addressed himself to that problem, and he did so again in September of that year in a piece for the *Elementary School Journal.* Teachers were reassured by Gray's research evidence, which was described by a writer in the *Reading Teacher* as a "veritable storehouse of ammunition."

In the year of Flesch, another important event took place. Gray and his colleagues decided to combine the National Association for Remedial Teaching and the International Council for the Improvement of Reading Instruction to form one major professional organization: the International Reading Association (IRA). It would, in a few short years, become the impregnable citadel of the whole-word method. Gray, as expected, was elected its first president.

In 1956 the IRA had 7,000 members; today, it has about 65,000. It publishes four journals and holds an annual convention that attracts as many as 13,000 registrants. In addition, many of its state organizations hold annual local conventions of their own. So if you've wondered why reading instruction in America has not gotten better since the publication of *Why Johnny Can't Read*, there's the answer. The profession is simply too well insulated from public or parental pressures. As long as the schools continue to buy the books that the professors write, why change anything?

Meanwhile, in those twenty-five years, criticism of the whole-word method has continued unabated. Charles Walcutt's *Tomorrow's Illiterates* appeared in 1961; Arthur Trace's *Reading Without Dick and Jane*, in 1965. The Council for Basic Education was founded in 1958 by a group of concerned academicians who advocated a return to phonics, and the Reading Reform Foundation was organized in 1961. My own book, *The New Illiterates*, was published in 1973. But compared to the IRA, the combined opposition is like a swarm of flies on the back of an elephant.

Despite the furor among parents raised by Flesch's book in 1955, no major publisher brought out a phonics-based reading instruction program until 1963, when three publishers — Lippincott, Open Court, and the Economy Company — entered the market with the new phonics programs. But the big companies — Scott, Foresman; Macmillan; Ginn; Harper & Row; Houghton Mifflin; American Book Company; etc. — continued to publish and aggressively sell their whole-word programs to about 85% of the primary school market.

Then, in 1967, a book was published that caused the IRA a bit of a problem. The book, *Learning to Read: The Great Debate*, was written by Dr. Jeanne Chall, a respected member of the IRA and a professor of education at the Harvard Graduate School of Education. After several years of research into a mountain of studies done on beginning reading instruction, Chall came to the conclusion that the phonics, or code, approach produced better readers than the whole-word method. In short, it was a vindication of what Rudolf Flesch had asserted twelve years earlier.

Since the book, financed by a grant from the Carnegie Corporation, had been written for the educational rather than the popular market, it did not make the kind of waves in the general press that Flesch's book did. Still, Chall had given ammunition to the IRS's worst enemies, and the profession dealt with her in its own way. The reviewer in the IRA's *Journal of Reading* (Jan. 1969) wrote:

> What prevents Chall's study from achieving respectability is that many of her conclusions are derived from a consideration of studies that were ill-conceived, incomplete and lacking in the essentials

> of suitable methodological criteria. In her eagerness to clarify these studies she allowed her personal bias toward a code emphasis to color her interpretations of the data....
>
> It seems rather odd that a researcher intent upon dispelling confusion should have allowed herself to be moored on a reef of inconclusiveness and insubstantiality.

Reviewers in the *Reading Teacher, Elementary English,* and *Grade Teacher* were just as critical, all of which seriously reduced the impact that Chall's findings could have had on teachers of reading.

Meanwhile, whole-word authors found it necessary to come up with new arguments to counter potential competition from the phonics-based textbooks entering the market in the mid-60s. The argument they used most effectively was that "research" had shown that there is no one best way to teach reading to all children. Or course, debating *this* took the focus off debating particular methods. Adding to the academic confusion in reading pedagogy was an expansion of the pedagogic vocabulary with the new terms borrowed from linguistics and elsewhere, sometimes to convey new concepts, at other times to obfuscate the obvious. The linguists, for example, reaffirmed the alphabetic principle underlying written English but came out strongly against teaching children to articulate the isolated sounds.

A new level of sophistication in whole-word pedagogy was reached in 1967. Professor Kenneth S.

Goodman, the Scott, Foresman editor who inherited William S. Gray's mantle of leadership, published his controversial article, "Reading: A Psycholinguistic Guessing Game," in the May 1967 *Journal of the Reading Specialist*. It was, for all practical purposes, an attempt by a professor-of-education, whole-word author to discredit the new phonics competition from Lippincott. Goodman wrote:

> The teacher's manual of the Lippincott *Basic Reading* incorporates a letter by letter varians in the justification of its reading approach: "In short, following this program the child learns from the beginning to see words as the most skillful reader sees them...as whole images of complete words with all their letters."
>
> In place of this misconception, I offer this: "Reading is a selective process. It involves partial use of available language cues selected from perceptual input on the basis of the reader's expectation. As this partial information is processed, tentative decisions are made to be confirmed, rejected or refined as reading progresses." More simply stated, reading is a psycholinguistic guessing game.

So a whole-word author was willing to proclaim that reading is a guessing game, albeit a "psycholinguistic" one. But is it? The alphabet, in fact, makes guessing in reading unnecessary. Once you are trained in translating written sound symbols into the exact spoken language the symbols represent, precision in reading becomes automatic. You might not understand all the words you read, but that will be the case with all readers throughout their lives. Yet here were children being deliberately taught reading as a *guessing game*.

Throwing Money at the Problem

Meanwhile, Congress had decided to do something about the reading problem in the only way it knows how: by throwing money at it. It passed the Elementary and Secondary Education Act of 1965 with its now-famous Title One compensatory education program. The new Title One bureaucracy began showering the schools of America with billions of dollars in the hope that students who were failing in reading would be saved from future lives as functional illiterates. But what actually happened is that the 17,000 school districts that got the money indulged in an orgy of spending and hiring that caused untold joy among the suppliers and new levels of prosperity for the establishment.

But did the program do any good for the kids? If it did, then we should have seen an improvement in reading scores by 1975. Ten years ought to be enough time in which to test the effectiveness of a federal program. But the results were dismally disappointing. From New York to California came the same disastrous news of declining reading scores. As for SAT scores, they were in an alarming nosedive. The *Boston Globe* of August 29, 1976, described it as "a prolonged and broad-scale decline unequaled in US history. The downward spiral, which affects many other subject areas as well, began abruptly in the mid-1960s and shows no signs of bottoming out." The verbal SAT mean score had gone from 467 in 1966-67 to 424 in 1980.

Anyone intimately acquainted with the reading-instruction scene could have predicted as much, for the federal billions did absolutely nothing to correct the teaching-methods problem. In fact, it aggravated the problem by literally forcing the schools to finance even more educational malpractice than they could have ever afforded on their own.

The failure of Title One to improve reading skills did not go entirely unnoticed. In 1969 the National Academy of Education appointed a blue-ribbon Committee on Reading to study the nation's illiteracy problem and recommend ways to solve it. In its report in 1975, the committee had this to say about Title One:

> It is not cynical to suggest that the chief beneficiaries of the Elementary and Secondary Education Act (ESEA) have been members of school systems — both professional and paraprofessional — for whom new jobs were created. Seven years and as many billion dollars later, the children of the poor have not been "compensated" as clearly as the employees of the school system through this investment.

The committee recommended a rather radical idea, a sort of reading stamps program — the use of vouchers with which students could purchase reading instruction from competent public or nonpublic courses. The committee wrote:

> We believe that an effective national reading effort should bypass the existing education macrostructure. At a minimum, it should provide alternatives to that structure. That is, the planning, implementing, and

> discretionary powers of budgeting should not rest with those most likely to have a vested interest in maintaining the status quo, especially given their unpromising "track record."

What the committee was telling us, in effect, is that the greatest obstacle to literacy in America is our own educational establishment and that if we want to achieve real education in our country, we shall have to circumvent that establishment.

What a staggering indictment! The system had been created to ensure literacy for all. Now we were being told that it was an obstacle. How could you circumvent $100 billion worth of institutionalized malpractice? It was more easily said than done. Actually, in 1975, there was already in operation a federal program that was making a very discrete effort to circumvent the establishment. It had been launched in 1970 by the U.S. Commissioner of Education, James E. Allen, Jr. as the Right-to-Read program. Its purpose was to mobilize a national commitment to literacy somewhat in the same spirit that the nation had mobilized its talents and technology to put a man on the moon, but with much less money.

That such a program was even needed when Title One was already supplementing the schools with billions of dollars in reading programs merely dramatized the utter failure of Title One. Of course, the International Reading Association was first in line to welcome the new program, which meant more money in the pockets of publishers and reading specialists.

But you can't fool all of the people all of the time. Indeed, some bureaucrats are honest individuals trapped in a system they cannot change. I found such a one in Joseph Tremont, director of Right-to-Read in Massachusetts from 1973 to 1980. Tremont had entered the teaching profession in the late 50s with much youthful idealism. He had taught in grade school and at teachers colleges and had worked with Dr. Chall at Harvard on her great research project.

In May 1980, a month before Right-to-Read folded, he told me: "I'm sorry I didn't realize the impossibility of all of this fifteen years ago. The irony is that I did everything I wanted to do. I did unbelievable things. But my superiors couldn't care less. They only care about the money from Washington. This is the most heartless bureaucracy I've ever seen in my life."

In 1981 Rudolf Flesch again put the educators on trial in a new book, *Why Johnny Still Can't Read*, an up-to-date report on the literacy scandal. But this time the reading establishment barely took notice. Kenneth S. Goodman, leading apostle for "psycholinguistics" — the new code word for "look-say" — had become president of the IRA in 1981, carrying on the tradition started by William Scott Gray.

If the nation wasn't all that worked up over what Flesch had to say, it was probably because people had already begun to accept declining literacy as part of the way things are. Besides, it was now possible to blame television, the nuclear arms race, or the breakdown of the family for the decline. Indeed, the reading problem had defied solution for so long that it now seemed wiser to adjust to illiteracy than to beat one's head against a stonewall.

If Flesch had proven anything, it was that the educational establishment was virtually immovable — incapable not only of self-correction but even of admitting that there was anything to correct. For parents, it meant that they could not depend on the schools to teach their children to read properly.

What Is to be Done?

It has become obvious to me that what prevents America from seeking a real solution to the reading problem is its mindless adherence to the idea of state-monopoly education with all of its aggrandizement of bureaucrats, its celebration of the mediocre, its oppression of the free spirit, and its strident anti-intellectualism. You cannot achieve high individual literacy in a system that numbs the intellect, stifles intelligence, and reduces learning to the level of Mickey Mouse.

So what is to be done? Since there is no national solution to the literacy problem acceptable to the educators or legislators, parents shall have to deal with the problem themselves. Many parents, in fact, have withdrawn their children from the public schools and put them in private ones where basic academic skills are stressed.

Most private schools, particularly the religious ones, where Biblical literacy is central, teach reading via phonics. But since many private schools recruit their teachers from the same pool of poorly trained professionals and use many of the same textbooks and materials found in the public schools, their academic standards may reflect more of the general culture than one might expect. Look-say, like television, permeates the educational marketplace so thoroughly and in so many guises, and it is so widely and uncritically accepted, that it takes expert knowledge to know the good from the bad, the useful from the harmful. The quality of a private school's reading program therefore really depends on the knowledge its trustees and principal may have of the literacy problem and its causes. It is the knowledge that can make the difference between a mediocre school and a superior one.

And in some cases it is this knowledge that inspires people to start a private school: to prove that the so-called uneducables are indeed quite educable. Such was the genesis of West Side Preparatory, the now-famous school founded by Marva Collins in 1975 in a black neighborhood in Chicago. A strong advocate of intensive phonics, Mrs. Collins started her school after spending fourteen years in the public system, where she saw children's lives being ruined by the type of noneducation so prevalent throughout the system. "We have an epidemic out there," she told a Reading Reform Foundation audience in 1979, "and millions of children are dying mentally from it. It's not swine flu, it's not learning disabilities, it's not dyslexia — it's the look-say syndrome. No one has found a cure for the look-say syndrome except the relatively few of us who are trying to spread the truth."

Unfortunately, Marva Collinses are rare, and there are millions of children who need sane, competent reading instruction. Some parents have joined the growing movement for home education and are themselves teaching their children to read or hiring competent tutors. In other words, there are ways to escape the state-supported monopolists, but it takes strong conviction and some know-how to do so.

Meanwhile, the vast majority of American children are trapped within a system that is turning their brains into macaroni. It's a tragedy that this has to occur when there is no lack of knowledge about how to teach children to read well. After all, they did it for at least 3,000 years before the professors of education took over.

California's Reading Debacle: When the Incompetent Rule, the Children Suffer

A lady in Southern California recently faxed me an article about California's literacy disaster containing much interesting information about what happened when Whole Language was introduced in California schools in 1987. The article, "The Blackboard Bungle" by Jill Stewart, appeared in the March 1-7, 1996, issue of *LA Weekly*. Ms. Stewart writes:

> Since 1987, whole-language theory has swept California. At its further extreme are whole-language zealots who believe reading and writing are natural processes that children will pick up on their own without formal instruction if they are immersed in good literature and allowed to freely write without correction. The theory's basic principles have been institutionalized in the form of a widely acclaimed reading "framework" adopted by the state Board of Public Education that downplays the teaching of traditional reading skills. On the plus side, the era of whole language has ushered into California's classrooms the use of literature and popular storybooks, and has inspired teachers to push children to create their own handwritten stories. "The core

> idea of whole language," says one of its most vocal proponents, Mel Grubb of the California Literature Project at Cal State Dominguez Hills, "is that children no longer are forced to learn skills that are disembodied from the experience of reading a story. The enjoyment and the wonder of the story are absorbed just as the skills are absorbed."

Poor Mr. Grubb seems to be confused about the difference between reading a story and learning to read. Apparently he thinks both are the same. Ms. Stewart continues:

> But whole language, which sounds so promising when described by its proponents, has proved to be a near disaster when applied to — and by — real people. In the eight years since whole language first appeared in the state's grade schools, California's fourth-grade reading scores have plummeted to near the bottom nationally, according to the National Assessment of Educational Progress (NAEP). Indeed, California's fourth-graders are now such poor readers that only the children in Louisiana and Guam — both hampered by pitifully backward educational systems — get worse reading scores.

And who is to blame for this "near disaster"— which is not near but actual? The article states:

> It has become clear that many of the problems stem from a tragic misinterpretation of the state's 1989 reading framework, intended as a helpful supplement to traditional lessons but used by many administrators as a wholesale replacement for them.

Was it, indeed, a "tragic" misinterpretation or a deliberate misinterpretation? In 1987, California already had a horrendous reading problem. An article from the *San Francisco Examiner*, reprinted in the *Patriot Ledger* (Quincy, MA) of November 18, 1987, states:

> Almost one in six adults in California is "functionally illiterate," and most of those who can't read are native English speakers who went to school in the United States, according to a new study by the state Department of Education. The report says 3.1 million Californians can't read well enough to understand advertising in newspapers, simple recipes or job applications....
>
> "These people who might be able to read a simple sentence can't tell whether a lease they sign with their landlord is taking them to the cleaners," says Lynda Smith, a consultant on adult literacy for the state Department of Education....
>
> "It's a handicap people don't want to broadcast," Ms. Smith says. "There are people who can't read walking around in libraries carrying newspapers. They want to be seen reading."

So obviously, 1987 was a good time to change reading instruction in California's schools. Getting back to 1996, Ms. Stewart writes:

> The situation has deteriorated so far that former state Superintendent of public Instruction Bill Honig, who oversaw the creation of the 1987 reading framework, has distanced himself from it, calling the framework "fatally flawed for its failure to anticipate the whole-language overreaction."

Not only has Mr. Honig distanced himself from the fiasco, but he has undergone a complete conversion and now advocates a phonics approach. In fact, he has written a book on the subject entitled *Teaching Our Children to Read*, published by Corwin Press. But we warned him in our newsletter of September 1988, in which we wrote:

> Functional illiteracy will be booming in California in the years ahead if the state adopts the look-say basal reading programs it has already approved.... Because of textbook selection decisions based on ignorance, millions of California children will be condemned to lives as functional illiterates. Such state sanctioned educational malpractice will be doing more damage to more lives than one can possibly calculate.
>
> ... And so if parents in California want to make sure that their children learn to read, they will have to teach them at home or place them in private or religious schools with good phonics reading programs.

How is it that we were able to predict the disaster that lay ahead? And why is it that we who have this superior predictive ability are never called upon by the professional educators to help them make the right decisions? The reason is very simple. Stupid people rarely rely on people who know more than they do for fear that the smarter people will supplant them. And so, they go on making horrendous, tragic mistakes that harm millions of children simply because stupid people don't know or care what they are doing. Ms. Stewart writes:

> Says Honig today: "Things got out of hand. School administrators and principals thought they were following the framework when they latched on to whole language, and our greatest mistake was failing to say, 'Look out for the crazy stuff, look out for the overreaction and the religiously anti-skills fanatics.' We totally misjudged which voices would take charge of the schools. We never dreamed it would be driven to this bizarre edge. When I tell people that we never even say the phrase 'whole language' anywhere in the seventy-three page document, they look at me like I'm mad."

And so, maybe Mr. Honig was not as incompetent as he was ignorant. It stands to reason that when you become Superintendent of Public Instruction for the state of California and you decide to create a "reading framework" for the entire state school system, you'd better know something about what's going on in the field. The war between proponents of systematic phonics and those of the whole-word method has been going on at least since 1955 when *Why Johnny Can't Read* was first published. Is it possible that Mr. Honig was unaware of this war? He says he failed "to anticipate the whole-language overreaction." If that is indeed the case, then Mr. Honig was clearly unqualified for the job as Superintendent.

The new Superintendent, Delaine Eastin, is trying to correct the situation. She wants to combine phonics with the good part of whole language: rich literature and early writing. Meanwhile, the legislators in Sacramento are expected to mandate the teaching of phonics in the grade schools. But what about all of those teachers who have been teaching whole language for the past eight years and have no idea how to teach intensive, systematic phonics even if they wanted to? Are they going to be retrained? And what is going to happen to all of those nonreaders in the upper grades? Will they all be remediated? The sheer cost of the literacy debacle will perhaps convince the legislators that they ought to test out all of these new education fads before implementing them.

Whole Language Takes Over

How did whole language manage to take over California? According to the article it began in 1986 when Honig invited a select group of educators "to brainstorm about ways to set California on a new course in reading." Honig says, "I told them to dream, and to forget about any old rules that weren't working." And dream they did. Cal State Chico professor Jesus Cortez relates: "Somebody stood up and said that we were there to create a new generation of superior thinkers and readers and writers who would run the businesses and set the policies of the twenty-first century. Creating that new generation was the dominant theme from day one." Not only were these people incompetent, but they were wacky visionaries as well! Stewart writes:

> The secondary-school representatives emerged as natural leaders because they, more than anyone, were driven by tremendous frustration over skyrocketing drop-out rates, the hatred many

> teenagers expressed for reading, and the shocking levels of remedial reading required by California's college freshmen.... They also knew that something had to be done about beginning grade school reading, but they weren't sure what.

Hadn't any of the dummies read *Why Johnny Can't Read* by Rudolf Flesch or Professor Jeanne Chall's *The Great Debate: Learning to Read* or Sam Blumenfeld's *The New Illiterates*? Obviously not. Nor did anyone suggest investigating the many private schools where children were being taught to read quite successfully with a phonics program. They were just gung-ho on something new, anything new, as long as it sounded good. Ms. Stewart elaborates:

> "The group was charting new ground, and we wanted an inspirational document," recalls Jerry Treadway, a textbook author and a professor at San Diego State. "I remember specific meetings at which Mel Grubb and other whole-language proponents convinced everyone that there was no distinction between learning how to read as a first-grader and the way a mature reader would handle the printed word. We decided that until we got kids to deal with language the way it is used by adults, as a whole thought, our reading programs wouldn't work.... We underwent a real interesting perceptual shift in the meetings, and what we finally stated, almost derisively, is that with the traditional reading approach, the emphasis is on mere accuracy. We said, 'How absurd it is to care about individual words and accuracy!' Under whole language, the rule was efficiency of the mind: Get the

> meaning using the least perception possible. Skip words. Absorb ideas instead. At the time, it sounded great."

Am I exaggerating when I call these people incompetent? Not only incompetent, but obstinately so. Ms. Stewart elaborates:

> But tension began to arise over draft language that soft-pedaled the need to teach basic reading skills.... And the noted Harvard researcher and author Jean [sic] Chall warned the committee that it was ignoring major findings about how grade school children actually learn to read — by the careful decoding of each and every letter and word.... But Chall was completely ignored.

We wonder how many on the committee had actually read Chall's book. In any case, the committee went whole hog for whole language when Francine Alexander, in charge of curriculum, proposed that the state adopt *Impressions*, Holt Canada's controversial whole-language story book. The idea of replacing the boring old primers with exciting "real literature" is what probably enthused the teachers most about whole language. The article continues:

> Unfortunately, while the group pursued its ideas within this cloistered atmosphere of growing consensus, emerging research was showing that just the reverse was true about how children learn to read....
>
> But while Honig and many skills-oriented members of the framework committee relied heavily upon *Becoming a Nation of Readers*, which confirmed the need for intensive decoding training for small children, the rest of the committee members were in

> the process of rejecting such research. Indeed, many on the committee began gathering material from theorists who supported their evolving views against teaching skills. Looking back, Honig says, "It is the curse of all progressives that we are anti-research and anti-science, and we never seem to grasp how irrational that attitude is. This is probably our deepest failure." ...
>
> In the end, the committee produced a thick document that was adopted by the state Board of Education and praised nationally on talk shows. Official textbooks were selected that were mostly literature; the book chosen by eighty percent of the school districts contained no lessons at all. Schools were expected to follow the new approach, and compliance officers began appearing in local classrooms.

Compliance officers? Sounds like something out of a police state. We thought that educators are strongly opposed to anything approaching "censorship," but here we have compliance officers making sure that teachers don't teach intensive phonics. The article continues:

> The late 1980s and early 1990s were heady times for whole language. An estimated 20,000 teachers took in-service classes or learned the new approach from mentors. Others paid $650 to private trainers like Bob and Marlene McKracken, just two of a contingent of consultants who swarmed California....
>
> At California's seventy-two teacher colleges, meanwhile, a near-religious fervor took hold. Whole-language enthusiasts like Barbara Flores at Cal State San Bernardino began pushing the idea, via teacher-credentialing classes, that teaching phonics and other

> skills directly to children was actually bad for them.... By 1995, some 10,000 fresh new teachers had poured into grade schools, thousands of whom had little training in the usual methods for teaching reading to kids.

How much will the state of California have to pay to retrain its teachers to be able to teach intensive phonics? Will there be a retraining program at all?

It didn't take very long before the inadequacies of whole language became apparent. A grandmother by the name of Marion Joseph, a chief policy analyst under former state Superintendent Wilson Riles, found out by happenstance that the primary schools were no longer using primers. She contacted several teachers to find out what was going on. She relates, "I got, almost without exception, 'Oh my God, Marion, we are having a terrible time. The new reading method is not working.' If they tried to teach phonics or word attack skills to the kids who weren't getting it from the storybook and the invented writings, compliance officers came in from their district office and ordered a stop to it. It was terrible stuff, virtually a new religion, a cult."

Marion Joseph complained to Honig, and Honig began to talk to teachers and came to the conclusion that his reading framework had been "grossly misinterpreted."

In 1993, Honig was forced to resign after his conviction on conflict-of-interest charges. Ms. Stewart writes:

> In the end, a rudderless group of state officials were left struggling to interpret a unique and untested reading philosophy that they themselves did not

> understand. At the schools, deep divisions broke out as district bureaucrats began dictating bizarre orders to teachers and principals.

Meanwhile, teachers and administrators at Eagle Rock's Toland Way Elementary School in Los Angeles County decided to raise funds for spelling books since the state had not approved of any. Compliance officers got wind of what was going on and spent three days in Toland Way's classrooms observing the teachers. They were reprimanded for using spelling books!

Nevertheless, state education officials were dumbfounded in 1992 when the National Assessment of Educational Progress (NAEP) announced that California's reading scores were among the worst in the nation. Ms. Stewart relates:

> In response, a meeting of top state curriculum officials was called in 1993. There, whole-language proponents — including the powerful California Reading Association, the California Literature Project and several state officials — successfully deflected an attempt to re-emphasize basic skills in grade schools.

It was argued that teachers would "go nuts" if required to make another big change in teaching methods. However, in 1994, new NAEP scores revealed the depth of California's reading debacle. Grade school reading levels were in a free fall, with California's fourth-graders beating only Louisiana and Guam.

The result is that California educators have spent the last year soul-searching and commiserating about the failure of their wonderful reading program. The article states:

> Jerry Treadway, of San Diego State, recently became the most prominent whole-language proponent to publicly concede that whole-language theory was fundamentally flawed, even while several of its techniques, such as using rich literature and early writing, were good ideas that should be retained.... "I don't mind saying it has been a disaster, as long as it's clear to everyone that it was done with the best of intentions by a lot of really committed people."

But that hasn't stopped whole-language fanatics from resisting efforts by California's department of education to implement a new reading program which stresses phonics and spelling. In fact, it is more than likely that the state's teachers colleges will resist changing their reading methodology courses and will instead remain faithful to whole language theory and practice. Thus, new teachers will continue to come out of these colleges with little or no knowledge of how to teach intensive phonics.

All of which means that the public schools of California cannot guarantee that any child will learn how to read phonetically within that system. And so, concerned parents will have to do the job themselves by homeschooling or by placing their children in private schools that know how to teach reading.

In the end, when the incompetent rule, the children suffer.

The Teenage Suicide Holocaust: Is Death Education the Cause?

Over 50,000 American teenagers have committed suicide since the introduction of death education in America's public schools in the early 1970s. According to Education Week (10/31/84), there are eighteen teenage suicides a day in the United States, or about 6,570 per year.

In 1985, a half million teenagers tried to kill themselves (*Boston Herald*, 3/5/86). There is no reason to believe that this widespread death wish among teenagers has abated.

Teen suicide is now so common, that only the most spectacular tragedies get national attention. One such tragedy occurred in the spring of 1990 in Sheridan, Arkansas, where three high school students committed suicide within twenty-four hours of each other. The town, with a population of 3,200, is about forty miles south of Little Rock. According to *Facts on File* (5/18/90):

> The suicides began April 30, when a seventeen-year-old student, Thomas Smith, walked to the front of his American history class at Sheridan High school,

told one of the girls in the class he loved her and then shot himself in the head with a .22 caliber pistol as his classmates watched.

Later that evening, a friend of Smith's, Thomas M. Chidester, nineteen, was found shot to death at his home with a .45 caliber pistol, leaving a note that read, "I can't go on any longer." The next day, another Sheridan High student, Jerry Paul McCool, seventeen, was found shot to death at his home with a .22 caliber pistol. Police labeled the death a suicide, although McCool's parents insisted it had been an accident. The three deaths occurred in the wake of another suicide in Sheridan, by seventeen-year-old Raymond Dale Wilkinson, who had shot himself to death on March 28. Police said there appeared to be no link among the killings, other than the friendship between Smith and Chidester, and that none of the youths had been in trouble with the police.

Cluster Suicides

We are now all too familiar with these bizarre cluster suicides that have shocked and baffled communities all across America:

Jefferson County, Colorado: At least fourteen, possibly seventeen, teenagers committed suicide between January 1985 and April 1986. A study showed that "few of the victims had taken drugs or alcohol before killing themselves. Some had problems at school or with the law, but others were model students who participated in sports and had high grades." (*Rocky Mountain News*, 4/10/86)

Fairfax County, Virginia: Three Annandale High School seniors committed suicide between September 17 and October 26,1987. According to the *Fairfax Journal* of 10/29/87, Annandale students are a "very ordinary bunch of American kids.... Nobody really knows what specific troubles the Annandale youths who killed themselves may have been facing."

Omaha, Nebraska: Three teenagers attending Bryan High School committed suicide and two attempted suicide within a two-week period in February 1986. According to *Education Week* of 2/19/86, the students were "normal kids, not really involved with drugs or anything."

Leominster, Massachusetts: On March 27,1986, George Henderson, fourteen, a Leominster High School honor student, shot himself to death with a 12-guage shotgun in his bedroom. He was the sixth teen suicide in Leominster in two years, the third in that school year. According to the *Worcester Telegram* of 3/28/86: "Here was a boy not identified as being a child at risk.... There was no indication something was wrong... he was a good student, an athlete from a relatively normal family."

Bergenfield, New Jersey: In March 1987, four teenagers — two boys and two girls — committed suicide by carbon monoxide poisoning in a car idling in a closed garage. They had made a suicide pact.

Alsip, Illinois: Nancy Grannan, nineteen, and Karen Logan, seventeen, described as best friends and classmates, committed suicide in March 1987 by carbon monoxide poisoning in a closed garage.

School Officials Baffled

School officials and parents express bafflement when trying to figure out why these youngsters are killing themselves. Some psychologists have suggested that it may have something to do with low self-esteem. But many of these suicide victims are good students, good athletes, well-loved by their families. So why are they committing suicide?

Is it possible that death education is the cause?

Most people, including parents, haven't the faintest idea what death education is. A graphic description of death education was given in the *Winslow Sentinel* of 4/9/90. Winslow, a town of about 5,500 inhabitants, is in central Maine where people assume that weird subjects like death and dying are not part of the curriculum. You'll assume differently after reading this:

> Death, dying, funerals, wills and organ donations — pretty morbid stuff, but not for a group of Winslow High School seniors.
>
> They wrote their own obituaries and epitaphs, filled out organ-donation cards, visited a funeral home and talked about such issues as mercy killing.
>
> They wrote instructions for their own funerals.
>
> As part of a week-long seminar on death and dying, the sixty seniors learned to feel more comfortable about the issue of death — what to do if someone dies, what to say to family members of a deceased loved-one, how to prepare for the inevitable.

"It's the first time I'd ever been exposed to anything like this. Families don't talk about death," said Jennifer Erickson, who took the seminar as part of her psychology class.

"Because of this course, I'll talk to my own kids about death," she said.

Jeffrey Charland attended the seminar as part of his sociology elective.

"A lot of people don't have experience with going to funerals," he said. "It helped us to feel more comfortable about being around someone who has lost someone."

Guidance Counselor Cathleen Clement taught the seminar. She came up with the idea for the course when she was in graduate school, looking at different areas in which students need exposure....

"I wanted to (conduct the seminar) in a positive, upbeat way, even though the topic is morbid," she said.

Activities for the course included role-playing, in which students pretended someone had died. They went through the motions of dialing 911, making funeral arrangements, and either going through stages of grieving themselves, or helping another person through those stages.

In the process, they learned about the cost of being embalmed and buried in a coffin, as opposed to being cremated, and about the choices they have.

"We got a price list on everything, and it's expensive to die," said Erickson.

Charland said that while taking the course he has made the decision to be cremated when he passes on.

"I want to be cremated because of environmental reasons. It saves land and is a lot cheaper," he said.

The trip to Gallant Funeral Home Inc. in Waterville was neat, according to Charland.

Although the students did not see any bodies there, they did see the equipment and tools used for preparing them for burial.... The students saw the make-up, and learned that a hairstylist comes in to fix the corpse's hair....

Clement said the students never stopped asking questions at the funeral home....

Erickson said she wants to teach, probably high school sociology, and Charland wants to work in the field of psychology.

Clement said some students initially felt uncomfortable with the seminar, but eventually became less afraid.

Were Parents Consulted?

There is no indication in the article that parents were consulted about the seminar or were asked for their approval. Also, not all students react to death education as calmly as the two interviewed by the reporter. Some get quite upset. Death educator, Nina Ribak Rosenthal, in an article entitled "Death Education: Help or Hurt?" (*The Clearing House*, January 1980) wrote:

> Death arouses emotions. Some students may get depressed; others may get angry; many will ask questions or make statements that can cause concern for the instructor.... Students may discuss the fact that they are having nightmares or that the course is making them depressed or feeling morbid.... Others

> may have no reactions or feel a great sense of relief that someone finally is talking about the things they often felt they could not say. Others may become frightened. In fact, Bailis and Kennedy report that secondary students increased their fear of death and dying as a result of participating in a death education program.

Depression, fear, anger, nightmares, morbidity. These are the negative emotions and reactions stirred up in students by death education. Is this what parents want their children to experience? Is this what they send their children to school for? However, according to Ms. Rosenthal, simply because death education can cause such emotional turmoil and anxiety is no reason not to teach it. "Since death has been such a taboo topic, open and honest communication is essential. Such communication," she writes, "helps to desensitize students to anxiety-arousing items."

Desensitizing Children

Thus, the purpose of death education is to "desensitize" children to death — to remove or reduce that reasonable, rational, and useful antipathy to death that helps us preserve our lives. It is when children begin to see death as "friendly" and unthreatening that they begin to be drawn into death's orbit and lured to self-destruction. It's a phenomenon that might be called "death seduction," in which an individual is drawn irresistibly into a fascination and then obsession with death. The individual begins to hate life and love death.

Death Ed in Kindergarten

Death educators are quite aware that they are dealing with a highly charged, taboo subject that many children cannot handle. But that hasn't stopped some teachers from introducing the subject in kindergarten. The January 1989 issue of *Young Children*, published by the National Association for the Education of Young Children, carried an article by kindergarten teacher Sue Spayth Riley about her class' trips to a cemetery.

After a discussion about burials and cremation, one little girl says, "If I die I don't know whether I want to be put under the ground or not. I want to think about that some more."

A little boy says, "When I die I'm not going to be buried; I'm going to be flamed."

The cemetery visits deeply impress the children as can be seen by the bizarre games they invent back at school. Ms. Riley writes:

> Dramatic play after the trip deepens and extends the experience. On the playground the morning after this year's pilgrimage, I watched as several children in the sandbox improvised three gravestones by propping plastic frying pans vertically in the sand. The children then lay down in front of their headstones. When another child walked by, one of those in the sandbox called out, "Hey, this is a graveyard, you want to be dead?" Another gravestone was erected, and a child began sprinkling sand on the others. There ensued much arranging and rearranging of children and markers.

Another youngster built a large rectangular block building — a child's version of a mausoleum — with enough room for a child, hunched up, to get inside. Ms. Riley writes:

> This box-like structure was solid on all sides except the front where a baby blanket, supported by a long block on top, served as a door. When a child huddled inside, the blanket was lowered.
>
> When (the boy) called me to the block room to see his creation, Greg explained, "This is a place for dead people."...
>
> Observing from the sidelines I watched the "dead game" progress. One child at a time would be "dead," she or he would enter; Greg would lower the curtain.
>
> Greg then announced they were going to put some dead babies in the box. He placed several dolls in a large wooden crate, then put another small box on top with two more dolls laid side by side. He attempted to put the whole package in the "place for dead people."... "Too big, it doesn't fit," he said. He then transferred the dolls into two shallower boxes....

Obviously, Ms. Riley and the National Association for the Education of Young Children are convinced that these morbid experiences are of benefit to the children. However, the high incidence of teenage, and now even preteen, suicide seems to indicate otherwise.

The Power of Suggestion

Children are extremely suggestive. Recently, in Canton, Michigan, an eight-year-old boy was shown a suicide film in school, in which a child who is depressed tries to hang himself. Less than twenty-four hours later, the eight-year-old, mimicking the boy in the movie, hanged himself in his own bedroom.

This was not the first such suicide. In 1985, a fourteen-year-old high school freshman, an honor student with great promise as an athlete, hanged himself after watching a television movie about teenage suicide, *Silence of the Heart* (*NFD Journal*, February 1985).

As a result of these copycat suicides, the press has noticeably reduced its reportage of teen suicide. Nevertheless, the schools are increasing their programs on death and dying, making it virtually impossible for any child to escape the influences and effects of this dangerous, morbid subject. And parents, kept largely in the dark, don't even know what is going on. They send their children to school smiling and happy only to have them return home depressed and suicidal.

How It All Began

How did death education get into the schools in the first place? The subject began to be taught in the early 1970s after the 1969 publication of Elisabeth Kubler-Ross's influential book, *On Death and Dying*, based on her lectures to medical students and personnel. Since then, Dr. Kubler-Ross has lectured widely, spreading her credo that "dying can be one of the most beautiful, incredible experiences of life if it is shared with loved ones." Acceptance of death has become the central theme of her work.

This view is completely contrary to the Biblical view, which sees death as the tragic consequence of man's initial disobedience of God's commandment not to eat of the tree of the knowledge of good and evil. Through Adam's sin, mankind became infected with the satanic spirit, against which every human being has had to struggle. According to the New Testament, the coming of Jesus Christ provided man with the possibility of ultimate victory over Satan: forgiveness of sin, salvation, and eternal life after death.

Needless to say, our humanistic educators do not accept that view of death as the consequence of sin. They prefer to see it as a "natural process."

The Making of a Death Cult

In the 1970s Kubler-Ross became involved with a spiritualist cult in Southern California, led by a "spiritual healer" named Jay Barham who believed in "spirit guides" and practiced "out-of-body experiences." With Barham she founded a healing center called Shand Nilaya, "the final home of peace," which has also become the center of a religious movement.

Kubler-Ross herself has become the charismatic leader of a New Age death cult. According to *Omega, The Journal of Death and Dying* (Vol. 16, No. 2,1985-86):

> Kubler-Ross' religion is a new form of an old tradition of religious thought and practice, namely, the tradition of the mystery religions, which thrived in pre-Christian antiquity. The womb and the grave have been equated in mystery religions.... This is precisely the significance of Kubler-Ross' choice of death and dying as her primary consideration as a charismatic leader.

Death Educators Organize

In 1973, a group of death educators decided to organize a professional association, one of the purposes of which is to promote death education in American schools. The name of the association was the Forum for Death Education and Counseling. Its purpose was three-fold: facilitate communication and publishing among death educators; organize conferences and encourage networking; and develop programs to train individuals "in the theory, methods, and subject of death education and/or death-related counseling."

The first president of the Forum was Dan Leviton of the University of Maryland (1976-78). He was followed by J. Eugene Knott, University of Rhode Island (1978-80); David L. Frederick, University of South Carolina (1981); Bruce Bowman, Maryland (1981); Joan N. McNeil, Kansas State University (1982-84); and John S. Stephenson, San Diego, California (1985-87).

The Forum's 1985 directory listed 689 members, 494 (72%) females and 195 (28%) males. Members represented forty-three states, the District of Columbia, Canada, Netherlands, New Zealand, and Australia. In 1987, the Forum changed its name to Association for Death Education and Counseling (ADEC).

A Growth Industry

In 1986 president John S. Stephenson announced that the Association had now "achieved adolescence and is ready to embark on fresh territory." He said:

> The Association needs to become a household name similar to that enjoyed, for example, by the American Medical Association and the National Education Association....
>
> Visibility gives an organization the opportunity to make its case. It also brings us face to face with our enemies and that seems to be important in planning strategies. One reason death education apparently has not met with significant resistance may be due to the fact that it is not widely known. We need to change that and provide the public with an appropriate forum.

Public Ignorance

As of 1990, the public seems to be as ignorant of death education as it was in 1985. Meanwhile, the death educators are busily promoting their interests among fellow professionals. In an article entitled "Development Opportunities for Teachers of Death Education" (*The Clearing House*, May 1989), the author, Darrell Crase, an education professor at Memphis State University, wrote:

> This article reaffirms the need for death education and offers some methods for improving pedagogical skills of teachers.
>
> A task force appointed by the president of the Association for Death Education and Counseling... is charged to (1) carry out a study of the current state of death education in U.S. schools, (2) make recommendations for the ideal K-12 curriculum in death education, and (3) make recommendations for minimal knowledge, skills, and attitudes that teachers should possess before attempting to teach death education to children....

> ...Although we can assume that most pedagogical efforts are sound, recent examples have surfaced, depicting miseducation and ill handling of attempts to address dimensions of dying and death. Consider the following items from the *Dallas Morning Press*:
>
> "Some (have) blamed death education classes for the suicides of two students who attended courses in Illinois and Missouri. Other students have suffered traumatic reactions. Minimally trained or untrained teachers have asked first graders to make model coffins out of shoe boxes; other students have been instructed to sit in coffins, measure themselves for caskets, list ten ways of dying (including violent death), attend an embalming and touch an undraped corpse (Levin 1988)."
>
> There have been a few other examples of ill-advised instruction such as a quick, three-day, shotgun approach to death education (Mueller 1978) where young students were asked to respond to a host of potentially upsetting death related phenomena. A lawsuit was filed (Freeman 1978) on behalf of students who claimed damage resulting from inappropriate pedagogical techniques. Certainly mistakes do occur in many instructional settings and some minimally trained teachers may, on occasion, handle situations inappropriately. But let us hope that the above examples are rare and that effective death education is the norm in our schools throughout America.

Making Death Ed "Effective"

And so the death educators are more concerned with making death education more effective than investigating the possibility that death education, in and of itself, is a contributing cause of teenage suicide. The statistics alone should elicit some curiosity and interest, if not alarm. In 1960 there were about 1,000 teenage suicides; in 1984 about 5,000 (*Idaho Statesman*, 3/17/87).

What accounts for this steep rise? All sorts of top-of-the head theories abound, but why hasn't there been some honest, probing research into the problem? Why must everyone involved seem so dumb-founded and helpless? Millions are spent researching insignificant phenomena, but not a cent has been spent on this life-and-death problem.

Is The Debate Over?

Meanwhile, the death educators have been forging ahead as if the debate over the wisdom of delving into this taboo subject is all over. In an article in the NEA *Journal* of March 1973, one death educator wrote:

> "Death by its very nature involves science and medicine, social studies and sociology, psychology, history, art, literature, music, insurance, and law." Thus, death education can easily be integrated into any subject and permits classroom discussion concerning "the moral and ethical issues of abortion and euthanasia, and the spiritual and religious aspects of death and afterlife." The article ends with this justification for teaching about death: "Subject matter for today's education must have *universality*, must be intrinsically *interesting*, must be intellectually *challenging*, must have both personal

and social *relevance*, and must prepare students for life. We believe that teaching about death meets these criteria."

Parents Are Irrelevant

And so the decision to introduce death education into the public school curriculum was made without consultation with parents who have become quite irrelevant in these matters.

In another article in the NEA *Journal* of September 1976, the author, an English teacher at a Wyoming high school wrote. "The highlight of the course was our visit to a mortuary and cemetery.... Afterwards... a boy stated, 'The visit to the graveyard and funeral home really blew my head, and I *had* to talk and think about death.'" And another student commented: "After discussing it with others, death didn't seem like such a terrible happening."

The NEA's Active Role

Not unexpectedly, the National Education Association has played an active role in promoting death education. It pioneered in the development of sensitivity training and values clarification by sponsoring the National Training Laboratory, founded in 1948 at Bethel, Maine. It has promoted death education by sponsoring the writing and publication of *Death and Dying Education* by Professor Richard O. Ulin of the University of Massachusetts. The book includes an eighteen-week syllabus for the death educator. An article in the *Boston American Herald* of July 23,1978 states: "At the time [Professor Ulin] began doing reading and research, the

National Education Association, the publisher of the book, was looking for someone to write about death education. A friend who heard about the NEA' s quest matched the author with the publisher."

In addition, death education is promoted in a book on Health Education published by the NEA as part of a series of books entitled *Education in the 80's*. There is a chapter in that volume entitled "Death Education Comes of Age" by Kathleen Hoyt Middleton. Ms. Middleton writes:

> In the 1980's the subject of death and dying will become an accepted and essential aspect of the health education curriculum.... Journals such as *Death Education & Omega* can be helpful in keeping up-to-date on the issues.... Funeral directors in many communities are also becoming more concerned with their role as educator.

Ms. Middleton is the author of *A Conceptual Approach to Death and Dying Education*, a complete curriculum for junior high. She is also Director of Curriculum, School Health Education Project, part of the National Center for Health Education.

Uneasy Teachers

Death educators, of course, are aware that fear of the subject among teachers must be overcome. An article in *Phi Delta Kappan* of March 1974 states:

> It is considerably easier to know something about sex education as an adult than it is to have experience with one's own death. But at least we do possess value-clarification precedents in approaching the subject

> of death. We have the rich experience now of sensitizing adults to racial and economic discrimination, sex stereotyping, and other human relations problems. It should be possible to apply some of the strategies used in those earlier inservice efforts to the topic of death and dying. No administrator should be surprised to find that his staff is afraid of handling this topic, when he considers that research studies reveal similar fears among medical practitioners and even prospective funeral directors.... Surely the topic is too important to be kept in the morgue any longer.

And so, out of the morgue and into the classroom!

We have now had about twenty years of death education, and in that time well over 50,000 teenagers have killed themselves. In a year from now, another 5,000 will have committed suicide. Is it too much to ask of our "educators" that they investigate the problem? Reverend Rousas J. Rushdoony has written, "Humanistic education is the institutionalized love of death." We suspect that it is this unspoken love of death which is leading so many teenagers to suicide.

Junior High Freshman Kills Self

The death of Jodi Ann Grist, fourteen, of Boise, Idaho, on March 8, 1990 was judged to be a suicide by Ada County Coroner Irwin Sonnenberg. He said that Grist hanged herself and died in her home of asphyxiation. An obituary in the *Idaho Statesman* of 3/10/90 stated:

> Jodi, a freshman at South Junior High School, was loved and cherished by all who knew her. She brought

> so much warmth, joy and love to her family and friends. She had so many special interests, including a love for horses, music and reading. Jodi will be missed by all who knew and loved her — she was such a special, precious little girl. We love you, Jodi!

After Jodi's funeral on 3/12/90, Ada County Sheriff's deputies searched two carloads of young mourners coming from the funeral and found a gun. But a passenger in the car with the gun said no one intended any shooting and said the gun had been unloaded and taken away from a suicidal teenager for her safety. The unloaded .22 caliber handgun was found under the front passenger's seat and ammunition in the possession of one of the youngsters. No arrests were made. Ron Arnold, South Junior High principal, said the school has been offering counseling for students disturbed by the death. "It's kind of a cloud that goes over the entire school," he said.

Boy, Eleven, Hangs Self

The death of an eleven-year-old boy in Boise, Idaho, who was found hanging from a swingset in the yard of his home on April 15, has been ruled a suicide by Ada County Coroner Erwin Sonnenberg.

Timothy Merritt was found about 1:15 p.m. with a rope around his neck, suspended from the crossbar of a swingset. Merritt's mother and a neighbor attempted to resuscitate the youth while emergency medical help was on the way. (*Idaho Statesman*, 5/9/90)

The War Against Christianity in America

The origin of the war against Christianity in the United States can be traced back to the early days of the public school movement when Unitarians, Owenite socialists and atheists, and Hegelian pantheists vehemently rejected the mainly God-centered worldview of the founding fathers and sought to secularize education and substitute salvation through education for salvation through Christ.

However, it wasn't until the turn of the century and the rise of the progressive education movement that the war in America took on the militancy which characterizes it today. The progressives were, for the most part, members of the Protestant academic elite who no longer believed in the religion of their fathers and transferred their faith to science, evolution, and psychology. The scientific method provided the means to acquire unlimited knowledge of the material world, evolution explained the origin of life and man, and psychology provided a scientific means of studying man's nature and controlling his behavior. There was no need for supernatural religion in the progressive scheme of things.

Early in this century the progressives embarked on a messianic mission to change America from a capitalist, individualistic, believing nation into a socialist, collectivist, atheist or humanist society. They were motivated by the need not only to prove the nonexistence and/or irrelevance of God, but to deal with the age-old problem of evil: what causes it and how can it be eliminated?

According to the Bible, evil behavior in man is the result of his sinful nature. Man's disobedience in the Garden of Eden resulted in his fall from grace, his loss of immortality, and his coming under the influence of Satan. Only obedience to God's law and salvation through Christ can save man from the horrible consequences of his sinful nature.

The progressives naturally rejected this explanation which, to them, was little more than mythology and fairy tale. To them, there was no God, and man was merely an animal, a product of evolution, neither innately good nor evil. The causes of evil, they believed, were ignorance, poverty and social injustice, and once these were eliminated, a just, crime-free, utopian society was possible.

All that had to be done was to identify the causes of social injustice, and a scientific cure to man's social ills could be contrived. According to the progressives, it was our capitalistic, free enterprise economic system with its emphasis on private property and individualism which caused social injustice. And underpinning all of this was the Christian religion with its libelous view of human nature, its emphasis on the supremacy of God's law over man's law, its support of the notion of unalienable rights and private property.

Thus, the progressives declared war on Christianity. Why? Because it posed the most formidable obstacle to their entire revolutionary program. But their aim was not merely to destroy Christianity, but to replace it with a new secular religion. In 1908 John Dewey wrote, in an essay entitled "Religion and Our Schools":

> Those who approach religion and education from the side of unconstrained reflection . . . are of necessity aware of the tremendous transformation of intellectual attitude effected by the systematic denial of the supernatural. . . .
>
> It may be that the symptoms of religious ebb as conveniently interpreted are symptoms of the coming of a fuller and deeper religion. . . . So far as education is concerned, those who believe in religion as a natural expression of human experience must devote themselves to the development of the ideas of life which lie implicit in our still new science and our still newer democracy. . . . It is their business to do what they can to prevent all public educational agencies from being employed in ways which inevitably impede the recognition of the spiritual import of science and democracy, and hence of that type of religion which will be the fine flower of the modern spirit's achievement.

The war on Christianity worked its way downward, from the graduate schools of education and psychology where John Dewey and his colleagues trained the future educators, until finally it reached the local schools through the new teachers, administrators and bureaucrats in the state departments of education. Christianity was eliminated in the new curricula and textbooks, and the new humanist religion was inserted in its place.

With the help of the courts and the American Civil Liberties Union the humanists have been able to eliminate from the public school virtually every manifestation of Christianity: school prayer, silent or vocal; grace before meals; Bible study; references to Christianity in school art or decoration; benedictions at graduation; Christian stories and themes in textbooks.

The current battle is over "equal access" — whether Christians even have the right to exercise religious freedom during extracurricular activity or use public school facilities for religious purposes after school hours.

Nor have the humanists limited their war on Christianity to the public school. They have embarked on a long-range campaign to expunge Christianity from all government institutions and to bring Christian children under their control in private and homeschools.

The humanists do not want freedom of religion; they want freedom from religion, and any public manifestation of Christianity is in their eyes an affront to their atheist sensibilities.

When seen in this context, it is quite easy to understand the anti-Christian character of public education and the proliferation of court cases involving religion in the schools. The humanists are on the offensive and advancing slowly and steadily, while Christians are fighting defensively, but retreating on virtually every front. Christians have lost the war in public education and are now trying to stem the assault on private church schools and institutions.

But the humanists have done more than simply eliminate Christianity from the public schools. They've erected mammoth fortresses of humanist culture in the state universities and colleges all across America. These fortresses are protected from Christian influence by the judicial doctrine of the "separation of church and state."

The humanists have also captured many private universities and colleges originally founded by churches and denominations. And even the churches themselves have been heavily influenced by humanist ideology.

In other words, we are really in the final stages of this long war. *But the war is by no means over*. In fact, Christian resistance is finally beginning to take shape, and the possibility of a Christian counter-offensive becomes more plausible for a variety of reasons:

1. The growth of the Christian Reconstruction movement, an awakening to the virtues of the Calvinist worldview which is providing the strong backbone needed to resist humanist tyranny and reconstruct society on a Christian foundation.

2. The growing separation of fundamentalist Christians from the humanist culture and the

establishment of new Christian churches, schools, colleges, and universities.

3. The growth of the Christian homeschool movement, which is strengthening the Christian family in an era of moral disintegration.

4. The anti-abortion movement with its increasing pressures on the judiciary and medical profession; the defeat of the Equal Rights Amendment.

5. The bankruptcy of humanist morality and the social anarchy it has created — causing in its wake tremendous disillusionment among many humanists and non-Christians.

6. The growing recognition among many non-Christians that a final humanist victory will mean an end to American freedom as we've known it for two hundred years.

7. The growing AIDS plague which will put a stop to the humanist sexual revolution and awaken Americans to the realization that "the wages of sin is death."

Thus, there is plenty of reason for hope. But the nation will inevitably go through some very trying times, and Christians may very well suffer more defeats before the situation turns in their favor.

The Strange, Irrational World of American Primary Education

In the last twenty years or so, I have done a good deal of writing on American primary education, and in the last few years I have begun to detect a rather sinister pattern in all that was and is being done and advocated by the educators. They seem to be teaching everything in reverse. For example, in reading, they insist on teaching children to read whole words if not whole stories before they have learned the sounds of the letters. This is clearly a reversal of sequence which makes no sense and, in fact, creates enormous learning problems for the students. So why is it being done?

Then on the matter of writing, I observed that children were being taught to print before being taught cursive writing. The problem with this sequence is that learning to print ball-and-stick first creates obstacles to the development of a good cursive script, while learning cursive first in no way poses a problem to learning to print well at any time afterwards. Obviously, the proper sequence in teaching handwriting, or penmanship as it as once called, is cursive first, print later. That's the only way to prevent the development of writing habits that make a transition to cursive very difficult, if not impossible. That's the way we were taught back in 1931 in the public schools of New York City. Clearly, the educators have reversed the proper sequence and the result is poor handwriting for most Americans.

On the matter of arithmetic, we find the same pattern of reversal. The educators have decided that children should be taught the concepts of mathematics before learning the arithmetic facts. Again, the proper sequence is just the opposite. Children should be taught to memorize the arithmetic facts so that the concepts will become apparent as they develop the ability to deal with abstraction. Also, today arithmetic is no longer taught as the self-contained counting system that it is. It has been fragmentized and subsumed under the larger rubric of mathematics which includes geometry, trigonometry, algebra, calculus, set theory, statistics, probability, estimation, etc. The result is widespread "dyscalculia," the mathematical equivalent or version of "dyslexia." In addition, children are expected to use calculators before they have memorized the arithmetic facts. The exact reverse is proper, for if the children do not have the arithmetic facts in their heads, how will they ever know they've pushed the wrong button on the calculator?

It wasn't until I came across a fascinating observation made by Reverend Richard Wurmbrand in his remarkable little book *Marx and Satan* (Crossway Books, 1986) that it dawned on me what had taken place in primary education. Wurmbrand wrote:

> One of the rituals of the Satanist church is the black mass, which Satanist priests recite at midnight. Black candles are put in the candlesticks upside down. The priest is dressed in his ornate robes, but with the lining outside. He says all things prescribed in the prayer book, but reads from the end toward the beginning. The holy names of God, Jesus, and Mary are read inversely. A crucifix is fastened upside down or trampled upon. The body of a naked woman serves as an altar. A consecrated wafer stolen from a church is inscribed with the name Satan and is used for a mock communion. During the black mass a Bible is burned. All those present promise to commit the seven deadly sins, as enumerated in the Catholic catechisms, and never to do any good. An orgy follows. (p. 14)

In other words, in spiritual matters, and no doubt in other matters that count, Satanists do everything in reverse of normal, sane practice, and in the primary schools of America children are taught everything in reverse of normal, sane practice. It struck me that this was quire an extraordinary coincidence.

I am not inferring that the primary school teachers of America who subscribe to these perverse practices are Satanists. They certainly did not invent these new teaching methods. The methods were invented by the professors of education in the various graduate schools of education. For example, the major professors responsible for inventing the whole-word method of teaching reading and arranging its implementation were: John Dewey, who argued that the old method of teaching reading encouraged individualism and had to be replaced by a new method that encouraged collectivism; Edward L. Thorndike, the behavioral psychologist at Teachers College, Columbia, who equated children with little animals; Arthur I. Gates, Thorndike's protégé who created one of the first look-say reading series; Charles Judd, student of Wundt, who became head of Chicago University's School of Education; William Scott Gray, Judd's protégé who created the Dick and Jane books; G. Stanley Hall, Wundt's first American student who taught psychology to John Dewey and James McKeen Cattell at Johns Hopkins University and later president of Clark University; James McKeen Cattell who studied under Wundt in Leipzig where, as a twenty-four-year-old graduate student, he performed his famous reaction-time experiments which were to become the sole "scientific" basis for the whole-word method; and Edmund Burke Huey, Hall's graduate student who wrote the first authoritative psychological study of reading that advocated the use of the whole-word method.

Were any of these professors Satanists? Not that we know of, although they were all members of the Protestant academic elite who rejected the religion of their fathers and became atheists and socialists. All were imbued with the new psychology which, along with evolution, replaced religion as the focus of their faith. And this new psychology, through the work of John B. Watson and Ivan Pavlov, developed into behaviorism which made operant conditioning, based on experiments with animals, the basis of the new teaching techniques for the primary schools.

Does atheism, in and of itself, produce the satanic effect? It certainly does open the door to Satanism, although Dewey, Cattell, Hall, Watson, Pavlov, Thorndike, Judd, Gates, Huey, Gray, and their colleagues would have insisted that they were "scientists," objectively pursuing scientific truths. At best it was very slipshod science. Cattell's experiments on reaction time hardly provided the kind of certain knowledge that made two thousand years of successful teaching experience suddenly obsolete. (Cattell was also ingesting hallucinogenic drugs as a student.) And Pavlov's dogs were no substitute for human beings. In addition, we now have had more than enough experience with behaviorist teaching methods to know that, while they can be used to teach monkeys to press levers in cages, they do not produce the kind of academic results that American parents want for their children.

Which brings us to another important point. Those who reengineered primary education in America did so in order to carry out a political and social agenda that had nothing to do with what the parents wanted for their children. These were men determined to carry out a revolution, to change America, to change human behavior, to change human nature, to change our economic system, to change our values. That it has led to the total expulsion of God from the public schools falls in line with the thesis that atheist scientists, who also advocate abortion and experimentation on live fetuses, are doing the work of Satan. Wurmbrand writes:

> So from time immemorial men have believed in the existence of the Devil. Sin and wickedness are the hallmark of his kingdom, disintegration and destruction its inevitable result. The great concentrations of evil design in times past as well as in modern communism and nazism would have been impossible without a guiding force, the Devil himself. He has been the mastermind, the secret agent, supplying the unifying energy in his grand scheme to control mankind.

Is American liberalism — sometimes known as progressivism, socialism, or secular humanism — the latest great "evil design" guided by Satan himself? It was John B. Watson, who, in *Behaviorism*, wrote in 1924:

> Human beings do not want to class themselves with other animals. They are willing to admit that they are animals but "something else in addition." It is this "something else" that causes the trouble. In this "something else" is bound up everything that is classed as religion, the life hereafter, morals, love of children, parents, country, and the like. The raw fact that you, as a psychologist, if you are to remain scientific, must describe the behavior of man in no other terms than those you would use in describing the behavior of the ox you slaughter, drove and still drives many timid souls away from behaviorism.

In other words, in order to become a good behavioral psychologist, you must adopt a view of human nature much closer to Satan's than to God's. Is it really surprising that so many educators have adopted behaviorism as the basis for educational psychology?

Benjamin Bloom's Mastery Learning scheme is based on Pavlovian-Watsonian-Skinnerian operant conditioning. And that is basically the teaching technique behind whole-word reading instruction. This was confirmed in so many words by Harvard educational psychologist Walter Dearborn, a protégé of Cattell, who wrote in 1940 (*School and Society*, 10/19/40, p. 368):

> The principle which we have used to explain the acquisition of a sight vocabulary is, of course, the one suggested by Pavlov's well-known experiments on the conditioned response. This is as it should be. The basic process involved in conditioning and in learning to read is the same....
>
> In order to obtain the best results from the use of the conditioning technique, the substitute stimulus must either immediately precede, or occur simultaneously with, the adequate stimulus. As we have explained before, the substitute stimulus in the case of learning to read is the word seen and the adequate stimulus is the word heard.

Arthur I. Gates summed up the stimulus-response, associational technique of teaching when he wrote in his book, *Psychology for Students of Education*, published in 1923:

> Association in Informational Learning — Certain types of information are acquired by attachments of this sort. When shown a leaf, the child reacts by becoming aware of the object. If, while showing the object, one says the word "leaf" a number of times, the child will, at length, think of the object when he hears the word alone. Thus he learns the meaning of the spoken word; for the word itself is merely a

> combination of auditory stimuli, of course, not in the least like the visual appearance of a leaf. Next, we may show the object (or say "leaf") while the child looks at the printed word "*leaf*: With sufficient combined repetition, the child now thinks of the object when he sees the printed word. (p. 220)

We find the same idea expressed in 1917 by Professor Mary A. Grupe of the State Normal School, Ellensburg, Washington, when she wrote in *School and Society* (2/23/17):

> The habits to be acquired as quickly as possible are direct association between thought and the visual work, phrase or sentence, and rapid, silent interpretation of thought from the visual cues. Beginning reading must concern itself with recognition of words, phrases and sentences as wholes and as carriers of meaning. Klapper says: "The method of teaching reading in the elementary school must seek to make the eye so sensitive to meaning that in scanning a page it becomes as unconcerned with printed words as the ear is with auditory symbols."
>
> ...Oral reading is a kind of fetish which has dulled our sense of values. Silent reading is much more important and needs to be cultivated from the first. (p. 221)

None of the above sounds satanic, but the results of such teaching methods have served satanic ends by destroying millions of young minds in the process and inflicting on America a decline in literacy unprecedented in history. But what is even more revealing of satanic ends is not so much the theories of learning first promulgated by the behavioral psychologists, or even the early implementation of these methods, but of their continued use despite the overwhelming evidence that they cause enormous harm to children subjected to them.

As early as 1929, the educators were warned of the harmful effects of these teaching methods by Dr. Samuel T. Orton who, on investigating reading problems among children in Iowa, came to the conclusion that it was the new whole-word, or sight method, which was causing the problem. In an article entitled "The 'Sight Reading' Method of Teaching Reading as a Source of Reading Disability," published in the February 1929 issue of the *Journal of Educational Psychology*, edited by Arthur I. Gates among others, Orton wrote in a very cautious, almost apologetic way:

> I wish to emphasize at the beginning that the strictures which I have to offer here do not apply to the use of the sight method of teaching reading as a whole but only to its effects on a restricted group of children for whom, as I think we can show, this technique is not only not adapted but often proves an actual obstacle to reading progress, and moreover I believe that this group is one of considerable educational importance both because of its size and because here faulty teaching methods may not only prevent the acquisition of academic education by children of average capacity but may also give rise to far reaching damage to their emotional life.

That was certainly clear enough. Nevertheless, both Gates and Gray proceeded to publish their whole-word, look-say reading programs based on Pavlovian stimulus-response conditioning theory adapted to primary education by Thorndike, Judd, and others. The results were predictable. A new disorder called "dyslexia" became national news. *Life* magazine of April 10, 1944, published a major article on this strange new affliction, stating:

> Millions of children in the U.S. suffer from dyslexia which is the medical term for reading difficulties. It is responsible for about 70% of the school failures in six to twelve-year-age group, and handicaps about 15% of all grade-school children. Dyslexia may stem from a variety of physical ailments or combination of them — glandular imbalance, heart disease, or eye or ear trouble — or from a deep-seated psychological disturbance that "blocks" a child's ability to learn. It has little or nothing to do with intelligence and is usually curable.

The article went on to describe the case of a little girl with an I.Q. of 118 who was being examined at the Dyslexia Institute of Northwestern University. After her tests, the doctors concluded that the little girl needed "thyroid treatments, removal of tonsils and adenoids, exercises to strengthen her eye muscles." No suggestion that they might try teaching the child to read phonetically! The article concluded:

> Other patients may need dental work, nose, throat or ear treatments, or a thorough airing out of troublesome home situations that throw a sensitive child off the track of normality. In the experience of the institute these range from alcoholic fathers to ambitious mothers who try to force their children to learn too fast in school.

By 1954 it was clear to a lot of intelligent people what was causing the reading problem. *Collier's* magazine of November 26, 1954 explained it all in an article entitled "Why Don't They Teach My Child to Read?" by Howard Whitman. After reciting a litany of parental complaints about the new teaching methods, and the problems their children were having with them, Whitman wrote:

> Two basic teaching methods are in conflict here. One is the phonetic approach (known as phonics), the old-fashioned way in the view of modern educators.... The other method, which the modernists have put into vogue, is the word-memory plan — also known as "sight reading," "total word configuration" or "word recognition." It has the more friendly nickname of "look and say," since the youngster is supposed simply to look at a word and say it right out. He memorizes the "shape" of the word, the configuration, and identifies it with pictures in his workbook.

Whitman observed that many parents were hiring private tutors to teach their children to read in the proper phonetic manner. He interviewed one such tutor, a Mrs. Helen Lowe of Glen Falls, New York. Whitman wrote:

> Mrs. Lowe believes much of the trouble in modern reading stems from innovations made by professional educators while they were seeking doctor's degrees. Feeling they had to make some "new contribution" to education, she asserted they dashed pell-mell into newness for newness' sake, abandoning methods whose very virtue was their proven effectiveness.

"I start teaching the alphabet, what it is, and where it came from — even if it doesn't get me a doctor's degree because no one said it before," Mrs. Lowe remarked. "I tell how symbols were adopted for sounds. And then I start in teaching the logical, phonetic approach to reading."

"But," I interjected, "many experts have said that English is not a phonetic language. There are so many words which do not follow 'phonetic logic,' such as *bough* and *tough*."

"The word-memorizers have been harping on that for years," Mrs. Lowe replied. "The fact is that of the one-syllable words, the ones which children learn to read, only thirty-eight per thousand are not absolutely phonetic. The rest of the language is governed by workable rules and the exceptions are soon learned in day-to-day usage." It must be borne in mind, too, she pointed out, that children learned reading phonetically in American public schools for 275 years before word-memory became the vogue.

The major troubles Mrs. Lowe has encountered in rescuing of children from the schools of poor reading have been:

• A tendency to guess at words instead of logically attacking them. Having been taught to look for context clues, they sometimes come up with *milk* for *bottle* and *snow* for *cold.*

• A lack of exactness. This fault sometimes carries over to hamper children in other studies, notably arithmetic. Mrs. Lowe observed, "If you can look at *milk* and say *bottle*, you can look at *five* and say *seven*."

> • A habit of reading words backward. Neurologists have called this fault "mixed cerebral dominance," but Mrs. Lowe has traced numerous cases to learning to read from pictures. "They have never been taught to read from left to right," she explained. "When they look at a picture your eyes can wander anywhere. You can look from right to left if you want to. Do this with words and *was* becomes *saw.*"
>
> It is quite possible that the most logical-minded youngsters suffer most under word-memory teaching. Their minds reach for the precision of logical word-attack but become bogged in the guesswork of context clues and the illogic of picture association.

Of course, Whitman's article had no impact at all on the professors of education. They simply beefed up their defenses of look-say. And the following year, 1955, when Rudolf Flesch's blockbuster, *Why Johnny Can't Read*, was published, the professors circled the wagons and created the International Reading Association which would become the citadel of look-say practices.

But how did the professors deal with the reading problems they were causing? They attributed the problems to learning handicaps within the children themselves. In the April 1935 *Elementary English Review*, William S. Gray listed a few of the things that were wrong with children having trouble learning to read via Dick and Jane: mental deficiency or retardation; defective vision; auditory deficiencies; congenital word blindness, which he pointed out was also known as developmental alexia, congenital aphasia, dyslexia, congenital alexia, strephosymbolia, and inability to learn to read; cerebral dominance, also known as handedness, eyedness, ambidexterity, mirror-writing; emotional instability; constitutional, nervous, and emotional disorders. That just about included everyone.

Other writers added their own exotic terms to the growing lexicon of reading-disability disorders: binocular imbalance, lateral dominance, word-deafness, word-blindness, acuity dominance, sinistral and mixed manual-ocular behavior, eye-muscle imbalance, poor fusion, social maladjustment, personality maladjustments, directional confusion, eye maturation, minimal brain damage, axial rotation, ocular blocks, endocrine disturbances, lateral preferences, vertical rotation in visual-motor performance, perceptual retardation, dyslexaphoria, prenatal and paranatal factors, monocular vision, neutral confusion, sociopathic tendencies, ocular-manual laterality. One writer related the blood picture to reading failure, another related a child's first memories of accidents to reading failure. In more recent years, with the help of federal millions, the researchers have started investigating the supposed genetic causes of dyslexia.

The latest on dyslexia was reported in *Newsweek* of August 29, 1994 (p. 51). It seems that neuroscientists now believe that "dyslexics may have an abnormality in the brain's medial geniculate nucleus, which relays sound signals to the cortex." According to Glen Rosen of Boston's Beth Israel

Hospital, "In dyslexia, the brain is miswired for language and thus reading." The article states:

> The problem seems to lie in a part of the brain that acts as an auditory relay station. This medial geniculate nucleus takes incoming sound signals from the ear, encodes them in some unknown way and sends them to the cortex, which makes sense of them. Rosen, and Albert Alaburda and Matthew Menard of the Harvard Medical School, found that in dyslexics, the language-processing left side of this relay station had fewer of the neutrons that process fast, staccato sounds — such as ba, da, ka and ta — than did the brains of normal readers....
>
> The discovery that dyslexics have fewer of the neurons that process fast sounds is based on the brains of only five dyslexics and seven control subjects. "By understanding the biological facets underlying dyslexia, says Rosen, perhaps we can bypass the standard way of instructing the brain to read."

There is nothing in the article indicating the ages of the five dyslexics, or how they were taught to read. If they were taught by the sight method and their brains now show signs of physical abnormality, it is possible that the sight method itself is responsible for this development. There is no reason not to believe that a teaching method that cripples a child's intellectual development may also produce a serious physical impairment in the brain. That would certainly account for why some dyslexics are so difficult to remediate, particularly if the dyslexic was a very obedient student doing everything in his or her power to accept the illogic being taught by the teacher, even if it required twisting the brain to do so.

Are the educators aware of this? It is true that there are a lot of stupid people in education, but there are a lot of evil ones as well. Take, for example, William Scott Gray, the mastermind behind Dick and Jane. Was he stupid or evil? In 1951, when it became time to revise Dick and Jane, Gray knew exactly what had to be done. In fact, we can measure the incredible pedagogic failure of the original 1930 edition by the changes Gray made for the 1951 edition.

In 1930, the Dick and Jane Pre-Primer taught sixty-eight sight words in thirty-nine pages of story text, with an illustration per page, a total of 565 words and a Teacher's Guidebook of eighty-seven pages. In 1951, that same pre-primer had been expanded to 172 pages, divided into three separate pre-primers with 184 illustrations, a total of 2,613 words, and a Guidebook of 182 pages to teach a sight vocabulary of only fifty-eight words! How much more proof was needed to show that the look-say method was an utter failure?

In 1930, the word *look* was repeated eight times in the pre-primer. In 1951, it is repeated 110 times. In 1930, the word *oh* was repeated twelve times; in 1951, 138 times. In 1930, the word *see* was repeated twenty-seven times; in 1951, 176 times! In other words, the Pavlovian-Watsonian conditioning technique applied to the teaching of reading was not working. It was doing just the opposite: producing functional illiteracy.

As a result, did look-say die? No, it underwent metamorphosis into something called the psycholinguistic method, which then metamorphosed into what is known today as "whole language." Although the proponents of whole language insist that their brand of reading instruction is quite different from the Dick and Jane basal readers, the basic teaching techniques remain the same even though the texts have been changed.

Whole language is largely the product of three professors of education, Kenneth and Yetta Goodman, and Frank Smith. Smith's book, *Understanding Reading* (Fourth Edition, 1988), is probably the most widely read textbook in America by teachers of reading. It is a non-stop diatribe against phonics and no doubt ranks among the ten most devious books ever published.

As for Kenneth Goodman, he gave an inkling of what whole language was to be in an interview published in the *New York Times*, July 9, 1975 (p. 35). The article reads:

> A student learning to read comes upon the sentence, "The boy jumped on the horse and rode off." But instead of saying "horse," the student substitutes "pony." Should the teacher correct him? As far as Kenneth S. Goodman is concerned, the answer is a firm "No."
>
> "The child clearly understands the meaning," Dr. Goodman said in an interview this week. "This is what reading is all about." First, [Goodman] rejects the assumption that reading is a process of looking at words and sentences and then deciding afterwards

> what they mean. Instead, he argues, reading is a process of taking in data, making informed "predictions" about what will follow, checking these predictions as the reader goes and, if necessary, making revisions....
>
> "There is no way to process verbal data fast enough without making 'predictions,'" said Dr. Goodman. "The difference between a good reader and a poor one is that the good reader makes good predictions and checks them quickly."
>
> Secondly, Dr. Goodman argues that reading is not the passive receipt of meaning from the printed page but rather an active process in which the reader actually constructs meaning. He thus rejects the traditional distinction that most teachers make between "decoding" — or learning to translate letters into sounds — and the subsequent gaining or meaning from written words....
>
> Finally, he argues that children can learn to read in exactly the same way they learned to talk.

The inference here is that children really don't need formal reading instruction at all. They can learn to read the way they learned to talk. Of course, if that were true we'd have no illiterates. But that is the kind of nonsense that educators accept without question. For example, in *The Washington Post* of November 29, 1986, in an article headlined "Reading Method Lets Pupils Guess, Whole-Language Approach Riles Advocates of Phonics," we read:

> The most controversial aspect of whole language is the de-emphasis on accuracy. American Reading

> Council President Julia Palmer, an advocate of the approach, said it is acceptable if a young child reads the word house for home, or substitutes the word pony for horse. "It's not very serious because she understands the meaning," said Palmer. "Accuracy is not the name of the game."

That's the teaching method being used by our educational reformers, in conjunction with Goals 2000 and Outcome Based Education, to produce a higher standard of academic excellence! If you're thinking that there must be something more behind this nonsense than abject stupidity, you are correct. An article by two whole-language proponents in *Education Week* of February 27, 1985, gives us more than a clue. It states:

> The accumulating evidence clearly indicates that a New Right philosophy of education has emerged in this country.... [By] limiting reading instruction to systematic phonics instruction, sound-symbol decoding, and literal comprehension, and by aiming its criticism at reading books' story lines in an effort to influence content, the New Right's philosophy runs counter to the research findings and theoretical perspectives of most noted reading authorities.
>
> If this limited view of reading (and, implicitly, of thinking) continues to gain influence — the New Right will have successfully impeded the progress of democratic governance founded on the ideal of an educated — and critically thinking — electorate.

The idea that systematic phonics, or literal comprehension, or sound-symbol decoding pose a threat to "the progress of democratic governance" sounds so absurd as to be mind-boggling. The notion that the time-tested method used to teach our Founding Fathers to read is a threat to "democratic governance" obviously infers that what the professors of education want has nothing to do with the form of government the Founding Fathers gave us. So what we are dealing with is not stupidity, but socialist revolution.

But stupidity can't be ruled out entirely. For example, consider this statement made by author James Moffett in his book, *Storm in the Mountains: A Case Study of Censorship, Conflict, and Consciousness*, a humanist study of parent-school conflict in Kanawha County, West Virginia, in the 1970s:

> "God believes in the beauty of phonics," means that those who see themselves as God's spokespeople prefer phonics, precisely, I think, because it shuts out content by focusing the child on particles of language too small to have any meaning. In other words, what phonics really amounts to for those who are sure they have a corner on God's mind but are very unsure of being able to hold their children's minds is another way to censor books (unconsciously, of course) by nipping literacy itself in the bud. (p. 225)

In other words, Christian parents are using phonics to deliberately produce illiterate children! But since phonics was the prevailing means of teaching children to read during America's entire existence except for the last sixty years, all of those people who read the Bible and wrote the Declaration of Independence and the Constitution were, according to Mr. Moffett, illiterate. Yes, some of the opponents of phonics *are* stupid.

But stupidity in no way mitigates the tragic consequences of whole-language instruction, which will indeed create millions of intellectually crippled children. This is the crime and tragedy the education establishment refuses to acknowledge. What is even more disturbing is the fact that millions of Christian parents, who should know better, are putting their children in the hands of these charlatans to be damaged for life. Would that Christian leaders speak out on this issue and warn parents that they are committing a sin against God by putting their children in government schools where they will be sacrificed on the altar of secular humanism. Let us thank God that there is a very wonderful alternative available: the homeschool movement, which is saving thousands of children from the crippling processes of public education. But if you can't homeschool, then look for a private school that adheres to Biblical morality and traditional academic standards and methodology.

Outcome-Based Education: The New World Order in Public Education

As everyone knows, American public education has been in crisis for at least the last two decades. In fact, it was the famous *A Nation at Risk* report, issued by the National Commission on Excellence in Education in April, 1983, that called for drastic measures to be taken if the public schools were to be saved from further deterioration. The Commission said: "The educational foundations of our society are presently being eroded by a rising tide of mediocrity that threatens our very future as a nation and as a people." Then it added a comment which raised a lot of eyebrows: "If an unfriendly foreign power had attempted to impose on America the mediocre educational performance that exists today, we might well have viewed it as an act of war. As it stands, we have allowed this to happen to ourselves."

And so the calls for educational reform came fast and furious. Basically, there were two types of reforms called for. Conservatives called for getting back to basics, for teaching reading by intensive phonics, for strengthening all of the academic subjects, for greater discipline, more homework, etc. The liberal education establishment had other ideas. Besides calling for more money, higher teacher salaries, all of which they got, their view of reform included whole language in primary reading, invented spelling, no memorization in arithmetic but lots of calculators, a breakdown of traditional subject matter into relevant topics, and, above all, a greater emphasis on the affective domain, that is, more emphasis on feelings, beliefs, values, socialization, sexuality, group learning, group therapy, peer counseling, death education, drug education, etc.

Obviously, these two views of education are not only mutually exclusive but produce totally different results. The conservative approach represents a traditional Biblical worldview that sees education as a development of intellect and spirit. It sees the school as serving the parents who entrust that institution to educate their children so as to prepare them to assume the duties and responsibilities of adult life by teaching them basic academic skills and subject matter that will serve them in any field of work, in any career they may choose.

Although the conservative approach recognizes that the public school is a secular institution, it expects that institution to respect the Biblical religion that is the foundation of our society. When I was going to public school in New York City in the 1930s, it was customary for the school principal at assemblies to read a verse from the Bible. In my school the principal read the Twenty-third Psalm, and I remember being very much moved and influenced by that reading.

Vice Admiral Hyman Rickover summed up the traditional view when he said the following to a Congressional committee in 1962:

> [A] school must accomplish three difficult tasks; first, it must transmit to the pupil a substantial body of knowledge; second, it must develop in him the necessary intellectual skill to apply this knowledge to the problems he will encounter in adult life; and third, it must inculcate in him the habit of judging issues on the basis of verified fact and logical reasoning.... [The school's] principal task...is to develop the mind....
>
> Far too many of our teachers do not possess the intellectual and educational qualifications that would permit them to offer such a course of studies. There is an easy way out, and many of our schools are using it. They teach simpler things that are easy to teach, easy to learn, and more fun besides — how to be lovable, likable, and datable, how to be a good consumer, [and, I might inject, how to use a condom]. These aren't subjects you can grade, the way you can grade mathematics or science or languages, but they are good for hiding the ignorance of both teacher and pupil.

All of that was said in 1962, twenty years before *A Nation at Risk* was issued. Apparently the educators didn't listen to Admiral Rickover then, and they have no intention to listening to his counterparts today.

Why? Because the liberal education establishment approaches education with an entirely different worldview, a humanist worldview based on the notion that there is no God, that man is the product of evolution, an animal, that the purpose of education is not to create competent individuals who can stand on their own two feet and make it in the adult world, but to change society. Humanist education is basically messianic in its outlook. It not only wants to change society, but also erase from human consciousness any dependence on a higher authority, that is, God. You cannot really understand humanist education until you realize that it is at war with the God of the Bible, for humanist education is a form of spiritual warfare, not education in the sense that conservatives recognize it. That's why Admiral Rickover's common sense fell on deaf ears.

Outcome-Based Education, or OBE as we shall now call it, is the most radical educational reform designed to further humanist goals. First and foremost, it does away with every last vestige of traditional education, its methods, its curriculum, its objective means of assessment, its time frame, its goals. When I refer to the last vestige of traditional education, what I mean is that there is not much left to traditional education to begin with. The *A Nation at Risk* report simply let us know how far we had departed from traditional educational goals. The cry for "Back to Basics" was a popular acknowledgment of the fact that the education system had long departed from its traditional curriculum.

But Outcome-Based Education did not suddenly arise out of nowhere. It has been worked on and planned by humanist psychologists and sociologists for years despite public clamor for back to basics. One must understand that these educational professionals feel that they have a mission, that they are more than just government employees, that they are in every sense of the word true revolutionaries engaged in a true revolution. That is why humanists have never had any intention of getting back to basics, and that is why so many parents have experienced frustration in dealing with school superintendents and school boards.

Of course, the whole departure from the traditional curriculum started at the turn of the century when humanists John Dewey and his colleagues decided to use our public school system as the means of changing America from a capitalist, individualist, believing society into a socialist, collectivist, atheist society. The humanists spent the next thirty years revising the curriculum and the textbooks so that by 1930 they were ready to impose the new socialist-oriented curriculum on the public schools of America. One might call that period the first phase of the humanist reform movement. It was dominated by behaviorist, stimulus-response, animal-tested psychology.

The second phase began in the early 1960s with the emergence of Third Force psychology developed by humanist psychologists Abraham Maslow, Carl Rogers, Sidney Simon and others who tried to inject an emotional and spiritual component in the behaviorist mix. Since the goal of education was now defined as self-actualization, the emphasis was now on the development of the affective or emotional domain through such programs as values clarification, sensitivity training, situational ethics, multiculturalism, pluralism, death education, sex education, etc. Education was still viewed in its secular messianic mission of changing human behavior in order to change society. Naturally, academics, in the traditional sense, suffered, because academics now came under the rubric of the cognitive domain, programmed by cognitive psychologists who were more concerned with the affective aspect of cognition than its intellectual one.

So you can see by now the assault that traditional education has been under since the 1930s. In the meanwhile, Third Force psychology has given us a whole new educational vocabulary with such terms as change agents, facilitators, learners, critical thinking, self-esteem, cognitive dissonance, experiential learning, congruence, empathy, relationship inventory, interpersonal relationship, therapeutic change, social climate, self-actualization, clarifying values, respondent behavior, operant behavior, nonverbal cues, taxonomy, morphological creativity, behavioral objectives, group experience, group dynamics, affective learning, confluent education and many more.

All of this has been engineered mainly by psychologists who have taken over the education system lock, stock, and barrel. From 1900 to about 1940, you had G. Stanley Hall, John Dewey, Charles Judd, James McKeen Cattell, Edward L. Thorndike, and their protégés Arthur Gates, William Scott Gray, William Kilpatrick, Harold Rugg, George Counts and others, all psychologists or educators trained by psychologists who transformed American education in the progressive mold. In 1933 you had the *Humanist Manifesto* which set the spiritual foundation for the progressive movement. In the 1940s and '50s you had the strong influence of communist social psychology through the work of Kurt Lewin at MIT and in the founding of the National Training Laboratory in Bethel, Maine, under the sponsorship of the National Education Association. That's where sensitivity training was born.

In the '60s and '70s you had the rise of Third Force affective psychology and the proclamation of *Humanist Manifesto II*, which basically outlined the curriculum for American public schools. But the beginnings of Outcome-Based Education can be traced back to the 1948 meeting in Boston of the American Psychological Association Convention where a group of behavioral scientists decided to embark on a project of classifying the goals or outcomes of the educational process since, as they said, "[E]ducational objectives provide the basis for building curricula and tests and represent the starting point for much of our educational research."

In other words, you build your curriculum on what you want your outcomes to be. For example, if you want your student to become a humanist, you start building a curriculum that will turn that student into a humanist. You teach him or her about evolution, environmentalism, feminism, reproductive rights, sexual freedom, alternative values systems, etc. And you must provide tests and assessments along the way to make sure that the outcomes are being achieved.

Undoubtedly, the end product will be an All-American pagan who worships the earth goddess Gaia and becomes a Congressman.

Likewise, the curriculum of a Christian school is determined by the end goal, or desired outcome, of the educative process: a well-educated Christian steeped in the knowledge of God and His law.

The result of the scientists' deliberations has become known as Bloom's *Taxonomy of Educational Objectives*, a behaviorist classification of outcomes produced by a new curriculum that does away with traditional subject matter and teaching methods. The central figure behind all of this was behavioral scientist Benjamin S. Bloom of the University of Chicago. His taxonomy, which is little more than a humanist-behaviorist straitjacket for public education, is contained in two handbooks, one for the cognitive domain and the other for the affective domain. Bloom writes:

> Curriculum builders should find the taxonomy helps them to specify objectives so that it becomes easier to plan learning experiences and prepare evaluation devices.... In short, teachers and curriculum makers should find this a relatively concise area of remembering, thinking, and problem solving.... (p. 2)
>
> Equally important, the psychological relationships employed by the classification scheme are suggestive of psychological investigations which could further our understanding of the educational process and provide insight into the means by which the learner changes in a specified direction. (p. 3)

> A second part of the taxonomy is the affective domain. It includes objectives which describe changes in interest, attitudes, and values, and the development of appreciations and adequate adjustment....
>
> It is difficult to describe the behaviors appropriate to these objectives since the internal or covert feelings and emotions are as significant for this domain as are the overt behavioral manifestations.... Our testing procedures for the affective domain are still in the most primitive stages. (p. 7)

That was written in 1956. But by now their testing instruments have been quite perfected to do their job of monitoring affective change. Bloom continues:

> This taxonomy is designed to be a classification of the student behaviors which represent the intended outcomes of the educational process.... (p. 10)
>
> The taxonomy is not completely neutral. This stems from the already-noted fact that it is a classification of intended behaviors.... (p. 15)
>
> By educational objectives, we mean explicit formulations of the ways in which students are expected to be changed by the educative process. That is, the ways in which they will change in their thinking, their feelings, and their actions.... It is important that the major objectives of the school or the unit of instruction be clearly identified if time and effort are not to be wasted on less important things and if the work of the school is to be guided by some plan....
>
> The philosophy of education of the school serves as one guide, since the objectives to be finally

> included should be related to the school's view of the "good life for the individual in the good society." What are important values? What is the proper relation between man and society? What are the proper relations between man and man? (p. 27)

Note that the relationship between man and God is not included in the taxonomy. The book then outlines the taxonomy, or classification, of the cognitive domain. Concerning knowledge, Bloom writes:

> Knowledge as defined here includes those behaviors and test situations which emphasize the remembering, either by recognition or recall, of ideas, material, or phenomena. (p. 62)

A sample of the knowledge expected to be learned is given as follows:

> To develop a basic knowledge of the evolutionary development of man.... A knowledge of the forces, past and present, which have made for the increasing interdependence of people all over the world...knowledge of a relatively complete formulation of the theory of evolution. (p. 71)

These are just samples of the kind of "knowledge" the student is later expected to manifest in his behavior. As for the taxonomy of objectives in the affective domain, we read:

> Affective objectives vary from simple attention to selected phenomena to complex but internally consistent qualities of character and conscience. We found a large number of such objectives in the

> literature expressed as interests, attitudes, appreciations, values, and emotional sets and biases.... (p. 7)
>
> [T]he process of socialization, with its development of behavioral controls, is a topic with which the affective domain is much involved. (p. 38)

Bloom then points out that it is often difficult to separate the cognitive from the affective. He writes:

> Many of the objectives which are classified in the cognitive domain have an implicit but unspecified affective component that could be concurrently classified in the affective domain. (p. 48)

Which means that you can easily slip in some affective outcomes with your cognitive objectives, thus making it easier to obtain the desired behavioral changes. And, accordingly, this is better done at an earlier age. He writes:

> The evidence points out convincingly to the fact that age is a factor operating against attempts to effect a complete or thorough-going reorganization of attitudes and values.... (p. 85)
>
> The evidence collected thus far suggests that a single hour of classroom activity under certain conditions may bring about a major reorganization in cognitive as well as affective behaviors. We are of the opinion that this will prove to be a most fruitful area of research in connection with the affective domain.... (p. 88)

If you learn nothing else from this article than the fact that the psycho-educators know how to cause a major reorganization of values in the mind of a child in one single hour of classroom activity, then you've learned why it is so dangerous to put a Christian child in a public school. I know of an eight-year-old second-grader in Michigan who committed suicide because of a film he was shown in the classroom. It took only one hour in the classroom to change that child's life permanently. The taxonomy continues:

> [Psychologist Gordon] Allport (1954) emphasizes the basic reorganization that must take place in the individual if really new values and character traits are to be formed.... (p. 89)
>
> It is not enough merely to desire a new objective or to wish others to be molded in the image that we find desirable or satisfactory.
>
> We must find ways of understanding and determining what objectives are central and significant if we are to summon the appropriate effort to achieve these more complex objectives. (p. 90)

Everything in Outcome-Based Education can be found in Bloom's writings. For example, in his book *Human Characteristics and School Learning*, published in 1976, Bloom expounds on his theory of Mastery Learning, which is at the heart of the methodology in OBE. The basic idea is that most students can learn what the schools have to teach "if the problem is approached sensitively and systematically." What makes mastery learning work, says Bloom, is the feedback-corrective procedure. He writes:

> The feedback procedures typically consist of brief formative tests at the end of each learning task, which indicate what the student has learned and what he

> still needs to attain mastery of the task. Mastery is frequently defined as something approximating eighty to eighty-five percent of the items on a criterion-referenced test. (p. 125)

In Mastery Learning the pupil is permitted to take as much time as necessary in order to achieve mastery of whatever it is the teacher wants him or her to learn. In fact, the pupil cannot advance to the next task or learning module until the previous task or learning module has been mastered. This means that the pupil may not graduate until he or she can demonstrate that "learning" (indoctrination?) has taken place.

The problem with Mastery Learning is the content of material to be mastered. It is easy enough to determine whether or not a child has memorized a specific Biblical verse. But how do you master material in the affective domain, and how is that mastery tested? By prying questionnaires.

Has Mastery Learning been tried anywhere? Yes, it was tried in a reading program in the public schools of Chicago back in the 1970s. The curriculum, following Bloom's taxonomy, consisted of 5,000 pages of behavioral objectives. The five-year program turned out to be a disaster with reading scores plummeting. It was obvious that learning by "behavioral objectives" does not produce true learning.

The man leading the OBE revolution today is not Professor Bloom, who is now eighty years old, but a much younger and energetic psycho-educator by the name of William G. Spady. In an interview published in *Education Week* (December 1992), Spady tells us that while as a graduate student at the University of Chicago and a member of the admissions staff, he recruited as a freshman a student by the name of Jim Block, a "bright, intense, athletic young man." During the next four years Block and Spady became fast friends. After Block got his bachelor's degree, Spady introduced him to Benjamin Bloom. Block became one of Bloom's best graduate students and did much of the basic research in Mastery Learning. Spady says that he was one of the earliest to know about Mastery Learning because he was getting the data straight from his friend as it was unfolding.

Spady then moved on to Harvard to teach social relations and education. He also got interested in organizational theory. He says:

> So, when Block told me about the fundamental changes associated with mastery learning — turning time into a variable instead of time being a constant, and having what I now would call a criterion base for standards instead of comparative standards — I found the ideas theoretically compelling, and I took them immediately to the educational system level — because to me the fundamental barriers to making the mastery learning idea work were at the organizational and institutional level. So I said to Jim Block — I mean we literally made an agreement that day — "You fix the classrooms. I'll work on the total system."

And so, Outcome-Based Education was born. Note that Jim Block's Mastery Learning methodology would be the classroom mode of instruction, and

Spady would reorganize the entire education system to make Mastery Learning work. In other words, the systemic barriers to Mastery Learning that were part and parcel of traditional education would have to be removed. The plan, obviously, was based on the assumption that the traditional school was an obstacle to learning.

So, an entirely new kind of system had to be created to make behaviorist mastery learning work. If it failed in Chicago, then obviously it was the system that was at fault, not the program. Outcome-Based Education is the new system.

According to Spady, our present traditional instruction system (which produced the most literate nation in history until 50 years ago) is a relic of the industrial age, and therefore we need a new delivery system based on Mastery Learning techniques (which have no track record of success anywhere except in Jim Block's experimental research); the present school calendar is a relic of the agricultural age; therefore we need a year-round school calendar that sweeps our traditional two-month summer vacation into the dustbin of history; and the present traditional philosophy of education is a relic of the feudal age (because it fostered intellectual development, religion, and respected parental rights) and is no longer suitable for schools engaged in changing values. What we need, says Spady, is a total revolution, a paradigmatic change.

And Spady knows how to organize a revolution from the top, a revolution funded by the wealthy humanist foundations (Carnegie, Ford, Rockefeller), and planned by the graduate schools of education, the state departments of education, and the federal government. The new psycho-educationist elite will destroy whatever is left of the traditional system and replace it with an expansionist, New Age, holistic system of total control under the OBE label.

What are the outcomes being planned in Outcomes-Based Education? How do the change agents decide what the outcomes should be? Spady says:

> We are starting with what the research suggests about the future and we design down, or design back, from there. We're talking about a systematic process called Strategic Design: determining as well as we can from studying the literature and available data about future trends and conditions that our kids will be facing out there in the world.

Apparently, Spady and friends are quite confident that they can predict the future and they are willing to gamble that the future they predict will be there when the kids get out of school. But to base an entire education system on visionary assumptions about the future is not only foolish but dangerous. What students should be taught are basic academic skills as well as the timeless spiritual and moral values of the Bible that they will be able to use under any circumstances. The Bible has endured for over 2,000 years as the unchanging standard and guide to a moral, healthy, and productive life regardless of the different forms civilization has taken. Isn't it obvious that a Bible-based Christian education can serve children in the future better than any secular education based on predictions of the future?

But the visionaries of OBE have a different view. In Spady's seminar guide entitled Transformational Outcome-Based Restructuring, we read:

> The visionary purpose reflects the rapidly changing social, economic, political, cultural, and environmental context in which our current students will live. As a result, Transformational OBE is inherently future oriented and focuses on students' life-long adaptive capacities. It requires a fundamental shift in the prevailing paradigm of educational leadership, policy-making, priority setting, outcome defining, curriculum design, instructional delivery, assessment and credentialing, decision making, and implementation strategies.

The key word is "visionary," and success in the OBE school is measured in terms of how well the student achieves the "visionary higher-order exit outcomes."

What is an "outcome"? According to Spady, an outcome is "a culminating demonstration of learning." The emphasis is on performance, not content, on behavior, not knowledge. A "high-level culminating outcome" is a "complex role performance." Curriculum and instruction are geared to "what we want the kids to demonstrate successfully at the end."

Will the traditional subject-based curriculum be abandoned? Yes, says Spady, "But content itself can't disappear; we just develop a fundamentally different rationale for organizing and using it; one that is linked much more to the significant spheres of successful living rather than to separate disciplines and subjects."

In that case, how will history be taught? Spady's view is that there should not be a separate course called history "that starts at some ancient time and moves forward to the present." The students should "thoroughly examine current problems, issues, and phenomena in depth and ask why, why, why, about their origins and relationships."

And so if history is not to be taught in chronological order for what it tells us about our past, how will American youth understand the origins and foundations of America? The Bible is our model of history because it tells the story in chronological sequence. If young Americans are not given the story of America in chronological sequence, then what America is at present will seem like some sort of incomprehensible puzzle.

OBE is also strong on the affective domain, Spady's seminar guide states:

> Transformational Outcome-Based Education exists to equip all students with the knowledge, competence, and orientations needed for them to successfully meet the challenges and opportunities they will face in their career and family lives after graduating.

What are "orientations"? They are "the affective and attitudinal dimensions of learning" that deal with the student's emotions, motivation, "attitudes," and relationships. The wrong attitudes — the spiritually and politically incorrect attitudes will no doubt be subject to Bloom's feedback-corrective procedures.

A key premise of OBE is that, under Mastery Learning, all students can learn and succeed and that the school can control the conditions of success. In other words, time constraints will no longer decide how long a student remains in school. He will remain there as long as he has to in order to be able to demonstrate in an "authentic context the outcomes of significance." As the OBE policymakers in Minnesota said when Spady told them that not every student would be in school for the same length of time or take the same courses, "If they can't demonstrate the outcomes of significance, then we shouldn't be letting them out of school."

That may mean changing the compulsory attendance laws to accommodate this feature of OBE. Incidentally, the OBE people are also interested in taking control of the children as early as possible. In an OBE program called Odyssey Project being used in Gaston County, North Carolina, we read:

> The Odyssey Project describes a formal system of basic schooling for students ages three to eighteen with a developmental prenatal to age three component. The project will use an outcome-based education model that focuses on the knowledge, skill, and attitudes that students should possess when they graduate from Odyssey learning centers.

Why this interest in preschoolers? You have to go back to Bloom to find the rationale. In his book *Stability and Change in Human Characteristics*, published in 1964, he wrote:

We can learn very little about human growth, development, or even about specific human characteristics unless we make full use of the time dimension. Efforts to control or change human behavior by therapy, by education, or by other means will be inadequate and poorly understood until we can follow behavior over a longer period. (p. 5)

The absolute scale of vocabulary development and the longitudinal studies of educational achievement indicate that approximately fifty percent of general achievement at grade twelve (age eighteen) has been reached by the end of grade three (age nine). This suggests the great importance of the first few years of school as well as the preschool period in the development of learning patterns and general achievement.... The implications for more powerful and effective school environments in the primary school grades are obvious.... (p. 127)

We believe that the early environment is of crucial importance for three reasons. The first is based on the very rapid growth of selected characteristics in the early years and conceives of the variations in the early environment as so important because they shape these characteristics in their most rapid periods of formation. Secondly, each characteristic is built on a base of that same characteristic at an earlier time or on the base of other characteristics which precede it in development.... A third reason...stems from learning theory. It is much easier to learn something new than it is to stamp out one set of learned behaviors and replace them by a new set. (p. 215)

And that is why the OBE people want to get at the children as early as possible, to indoctrinate them before anybody else can get to them. Bloom also worked on ways of applying testing procedures to measure affective components in education and to keep track of the student's development over a long period of time. All of this has been incorporated into OBE data collection by computer, so that each student's data file will be available to anyone who has access to the data bank.

And what happens after the student has jumped through all the hoops and can demonstrate a "higher order competency in a complex role performance"? According to Hillary Clinton and Ira Magaziner in an article in *Educational Leadership* (March 1992, p. 12):

> Students passing a series of performance-based assessments that incorporate this new standard would be awarded a Certificate of Initial Mastery. Possession of the certificate would qualify the student to choose among going to work, entering a college preparatory program, or studying for a Technological and Professional Certificate.... Through new local employment and training boards, states with federal assistance, should create and fund alternative learning environments for those who cannot attain the Certificate of Initial Mastery in regular schools.

There you see the makings of a three-tier society tailor-made for the New World Order: a university elite at the top, born to rule; a body of technicians and professionals to keep the wheels of government, industry and the service economy working smoothly;

and the "workers" who will be at the bottom of the new caste system. Maybe that's why the OBE people have packaged their program so deceptively. Spady says:

> In January of 1980 we convened a meeting of forty-two people to form the Network for Outcome-Based Schools. Most of the people who were there — Jim Block, John Champlin — had a strong background in mastery learning, since it was what OBE was called at the time. But I pleaded with the group not to use the name "mastery learning" in the network's new name because the word "mastery" has already been destroyed through poor implementation.

Of course he was referring to the fiasco in Chicago. And since we have found nothing but whole language in the OBE programs now being used, there is no reason to believe that Mastery Learning disguised as OBE will do any better. And so the deception goes on, and millions of children will be subjected to more insane experimentation because a group of psycho-educator control freaks are determined to have their way regardless of what parents think or want. And that is why it is more imperative than ever for parents to keep their children out of the public schools.

And because the psycho-educators know that a large number of children will not be able to learn to read under mastery-learning whole language, they are already preparing American industry to accept that reality. It was Professor Anthony Oettinger of Harvard University's Division of Applied Science who told an audience of executives in 1981:

> The present "traditional" concept of literacy has to do with the ability to read and write. But the real question that confronts us today is: How do we help citizens function well in their society? How can they acquire the skills necessary to solve their problems? Do we really want to teach people to do a lot of sums or write in "a fine round hand" when they have a five-dollar hand held calculator or a word processor to work with? Or do we really have to have everybody literate — writing and reading in the traditional sense when we have the means through our technology to achieve a new flowering of oral communication? It is the traditional idea that says certain forms of communication, such as comic books, are "bad." But in the modern context of functionalism they may not be all that bad.

Now I wonder how many parents send their children to school to learn to read comic books. And I wonder how many parents ask themselves "do we really have to have everybody literate?" Of course, we do. That's why we have compulsory school attendance from age six to eighteen. That's why parents can be sent to jail if they fail to send their children to school. And why force children to sit in school for twelve years if you're not going to make them literate "in the traditional sense"? What other kind of literacy makes any sense at all?

But the key to Professor Oettinger's view is in the very question he asks: "Do we really want to teach, etc." What he really means is that the educators really don't want to teach children to read and write in the traditional sense, and even if they don't want to do the job that parents want them to do, they have no intention of letting anyone else who wants to do the job come in and take their place. That's the kind of situation we are dealing with, one in which parents have no say in how their children are to be educated, one in which parents are being outrageously deceived by self-appointed planners of The New World Order, one which no thinking, rational American can accept.

The Founding Fathers on Religion and Morality

It is indeed sad that American children today are not being taught much, if anything, about our Founding Fathers and what their vision of America was. Even when I was going to public school back in the 1930s and '40s, very little was taught about the religious and moral beliefs of our Founding Fathers.

We learned about George Washington as a great soldier and a great leader, but virtually nothing about his religious convictions. The same was true of all the other noted Founding Fathers: Jefferson, Adams, Hancock, Franklin, Hamilton. They were great revolutionary leaders who crafted the Declaration of Independence, fought a six-year war against Great Britain, crafted the Articles of Confederation and then the Constitution, which is the basis of our political system. Surprisingly you can teach a great deal about all of that with virtually no mention of religion, leaving the impression that religion didn't matter then and doesn't matter now.

In fact, we were taught more about the atheist Tom Paine than about any of the great American religious and intellectual leaders of that early period, such as

Jonathan Edwards, Timothy Dwight, George Whitefield, John Witherspoon, John Dickinson, George Mason, Jonathan Mayhew, Nathanael Emmons, Jedidiah Morse, Noah Webster, and others.

Why was this the case? Because by the 1930s the progressives were sufficiently in control of the curriculum so that they could carry out their long-range plan to remove religion from American public schools. Yet, in those days it was still possible for a school principal to read a psalm from the Bible at assembly. Of course, even that is no longer possible. In fact, the atmosphere in some schools has become so anti-Christian that it is forbidden to even mention the word *Christmas* within their walls.

John Leo in *U.S. News & World Report* (January 6, 1997) wrote that in Fayette County, Kentucky, school bus drivers were warned not to say Merry Christmas to any of the children, and in West Orange, N.J. a student was reprimanded by the high school dean for singing "God Rest Ye Merry Gentlemen" on school property. And the principal of Loudoun High School in Virginia told student editors to keep the newspaper as secular as possible and "to be careful that they don't associate the upcoming holiday with any particular religion." One wonders how they were supposed to do that inasmuch as the upcoming holiday celebrated the birth of Jesus Christ! Talk about censorship. I wonder what the ACLU or People for the American Way will do about *that*. But they'll probably argue that the intent of the Bill of Rights was to grant Americans freedom *from* religion, not freedom *of* religion. That certainly seems to be the rationale behind all of this undisguised anti-Christianity.

Some schools now allow only instrumental versions of traditional carols. The words are simply too controversial and violate the sacred separation of church and state.

And that's why the religious convictions of our Founding Fathers cannot be taught to American children in our public schools. These poor children no doubt get the impression — if they are taught at all about the Founding Fathers — that they were men with no religious convictions at all and that religion simply did not exist as a vital spiritual or cultural force in America when in reality it was the very force that made America possible. If they are taught anything at all about religion in early America it is usually about those mean, bigoted Puritans who hounded the poor witches of Salem.

Christopher Columbus

And yet, what the Founding Fathers had to say about God is so inspiring that I wish there were a way that American children could be made aware of this. It's easy enough for homeschoolers to get this knowledge. David Barton has written books on the subject, and there's an excellent book by William J. Federer, *America's God and Country, Encyclopedia of Quotations,* filled with wonderful and inspiring words from the time of Columbus to the present day, proving that belief in God, acknowledging His blessings, and working to fulfill His promises are the most important themes in the entire American enterprise. Christopher Columbus wrote in his *Book of Prophecies:*

> It was the Lord who put into my mind (I could feel His hand upon me) the fact that it would be possible to sail from here to the Indies....
>
> There was no question that the inspiration was from the Holy Spirit, because He comforted me with rays of marvelous illumination from the Holy Scriptures ...encouraging me continually to press forward, and without ceasing for a moment they now encourage me to make haste.

In a letter written in 1493 to Spain's General Treasurer Gabriel Sanchez, Columbus wrote:

> That which the unaided intellect of man could not compass, the Spirit of God has granted to human exertions, for God is wont to hear the prayers of His servants who love His precepts even to the performance of apparent impossibilities. Therefore, let the king and queen, our princes and their most happy kingdoms, and all the other provinces of Christendom, render thanks to our Lord and Saviour Jesus Christ.

The Pilgrim Fathers

In June of 1630, ten years after the Pilgrims founded the Plymouth Colony, Governor John Winthrop landed in Massachusetts Bay with 700 people in eleven ships, thus beginning the Great Migration, which lasted sixteen years and saw more than 20,000 Puritans embark for New England. In an exhortation aboard the ship *Arbella* before disembarking on the shores of New England, Winthrop said:

> We are a Company, professing ourselves fellow members of Christ, and thus we ought to account ourselves knit together by this bond of love....
>
> Thus stands the cause between God and us: we are entered into covenant with Him for this work. We have taken out a Commission, the Lord hath given us leave to draw our own articles....
>
> We must hold a familiar commerce together in each other in all meekness, gentleness, patience, and liberality. We must delight in each other, make one another's condition our own, rejoice together, mourn together, labor and suffer together, always having before our eyes our Commission and Community in this work, as members of the same body....
>
> We shall find that the God of Israel is among us, when ten of us shall be able to resist a thousand of our enemies, when He shall make us a praise and glory, that men of succeeding plantations shall say, "The Lord make it like that of New England."
>
> For we must consider that we shall be as a City upon a Hill, the eyes of all people are upon us.

That's the kind of religious fervor and covenantal love that permitted the Puritans to create a Christian civilization in the wilderness of the new world. And from that community came some of the most learned men of God that Christendom has ever known. Harvard College was founded in 1636 for the purpose of training up a learned clergy. And indeed it did. Increase Mather, who became President of Harvard, was one of the first to criticize the British monarch, Charles II, for demanding in 1684 the return of the charter which had given the colonists the right to govern themselves. He wrote:

> To submit and resign their charter would be inconsistent with the main end of their fathers' coming to New England.... [Although resistance would provoke] great sufferings, [it was] better to suffer than sin. Let them trust in the God of their fathers, which is better than to put confidences in princes. And if they suffer, because they dare not comply with the wills of men against the will of God, they suffer in a good cause.

Already one can see the seed of the War for Independence being planted in the soil of New England.

Jonathan Edwards

Jonathan Edwards, the great theologian whose preaching began the revival known as the Great Awakening, was the third President of Princeton University. Concerning the Great Awakening, he wrote:

> And then it was, in the latter part of December, that the Spirit of God began extraordinarily to ... work amongst us.... In every place, God brought His saving blessings with Him, and His Word, attended with Spirit ... returned not void.

George Whitefield, the famous dynamic evangelist of the Great Awakening, preached up and down the Eastern seaboard of America. Benjamin Franklin wrote that he was able to hear Whitefield's voice nearly a mile away. Whitefield wrote:

> Those who live godly in Christ, may not so much be said to live, as Christ to live in them.... They are led by the Spirit as a child is led by the hand of its father....
>
> They hear, know, and obey his voice.... Being born again in God they habitually live to, and daily walk with God.

Sarah Edwards, wife of Jonathan Edwards, wrote of Whitefield:

> It is wonderful to see what a spell he casts over an audience by proclaiming the simplest truths of the Bible.... Our mechanics shut up their shops, and the day laborers throw down their tools to go and hear him preach, and few return unaffected.

Benjamin Franklin

Benjamin Franklin wrote:

> It was wonderful to see the change soon made in the manners of our inhabitants. From being thoughtless or indifferent about religion, it seemed as if all the world were growing religious, so that one could not walk thro' the town in an evening without hearing psalms sung in different families of every street.

On matters of education, in 1750 Franklin wrote to Dr. Samuel Johnson, the first president of King's College (now Columbia University):

> I think with you, that nothing is of more importance for the public weal, than to form and train up youth in wisdom and virtue.... I think also, general virtue is more probably to be expected and obtained from the education of youth, than from the exhortation of adult

> persons; bad habits and vices of the mind being, like diseases of the body, more easily prevented than cured.
>
> I think, moreover, that talents for the education of youth are the gift of God; and that he on whom they are bestowed, whenever a way is opened for the use of them, is as strongly called as if heard a voice from heaven.

Franklin wrote in his *Autobiography* this prayer that he prayed every day:

> O powerful goodness! Bountiful Father! Merciful Guide! Increase in me that wisdom which discovers my truest interest. Strengthen my resolution to perform what that wisdom dictates. Accept my kind offices to thy other children as the only return in my power for thy continual favors to me.

Wouldn't that be a wonderful nonsectarian prayer for school children to recite each day? It is said that Franklin was a Deist. He had been brought up and educated as a Presbyterian, but he rejected many of the doctrines of the Presbyterian faith. But he writes in his *Autobiography*:

> I never doubted, for instance, the existence of the Deity; that he made the world, and governed it by his Providence; that the most acceptable service of God was the doing good to man; that our souls are immortal; and that all crime will be punished, and virtue rewarded, either here or hereafter.

In July 1776, Franklin was appointed to a committee to draft a seal for the newly formed United States. He proposed:

> Moses lifting up his wand, and dividing the red sea, and pharaoh in his chariot overwhelmed with the waters. This motto: "Rebellion to tyrants is obedience to God."

In 1787 Franklin wrote in a letter:

> Only a virtuous people are capable of freedom. As nations become corrupt and vicious, they have more need of masters.

At the Constitutional Convention in 1787, Franklin, disturbed by the bitter debates among the delegates, said in a speech to the convention:

> I have lived, Sir, a long time, and the longer I live, the more convincing proofs I see of this truth — that God Governs in the affairs of men....
>
> We have been assured, Sir, in the Sacred Writings, that "except the Lord build the House, they labor in vain that build it."...
>
> I therefore beg leave to move — that henceforth prayers imploring the assistance of Heaven, and its blessing on our deliberations, be held in this Assembly every morning before we proceed to business, and that one or more of the clergy of this city be requested to officiate in that service.

It should be noted that prayers have opened both houses of Congress ever since.

George Washington

It would take a full day to talk of the religious character of George Washington who was deeply conscious of his Christian faith. He believed that he was miraculously saved from death after a battle in 1755. He wrote to his brother:

> But by the all-powerful dispensations of Providence, I have been protected beyond all human probability or expectation; for I had four bullets through my coat, and two horses shot under me, yet escaped unhurt, although death was leveling my companions on every side of me!

As Commander-in-Chief of the Continental Army Washington often prayed and fasted, invoking God's protection and providence during the entire War of Independence. He appointed chaplains for every regiment. In 1789, at his inauguration as the first President of the United States, Washington said:

> Such being the impressions under which I have, in obedience to the public summons, repaired to the present station, it would be peculiarly improper to omit, in this first official act, my fervent supplications to the Almighty Being who rules over the universe, who presides in the councils of nations and whose providential aids can supply every human defect, that His benediction may consecrate to the liberties and happiness of the people of the United States a Government instituted by themselves for these essential purposes; and may enable every instrument employed in its administration to execute with success, the functions allotted to his charge....
>
> No people can be bound to acknowledge and adore the Invisible Hand which conducts the affairs of men more than the people of the United States.

> Every step by which they have advanced to the character of an independent nation seems to have been distinguished by some token of providential agency....

Washington's inaugural address should be required reading in every American public school. But, of course, all of Washington's references to God would send the ACLU and People for the American Way screaming to the Supreme Court that such an act would be a violation of the separation of church and state. That's how far we've come.

On October 3, 1789, Washington issued a *National Day of Thanksgiving Proclamation* in which he stated:

> Whereas it is the duty of all nations to acknowledge the providence of Almighty God, to obey His will, to be grateful for His benefits, and humbly to implore His protection and favor....
>
> Now, therefore, I do recommend and assign Thursday, the twenty-sixth day of November next, to be devoted by the people of these United States...that we then may all unite unto Him our sincere and humble thanks for His kind care and protection of the people of this country previous to their becoming a nation; for the signal and manifold mercies and the favorable interpositions of His providence in the course and conclusion of the late war; for the great degree of tranquility, union, and plenty which we have since enjoyed; for the peaceable and rational manner in which we have been enabled to establish constitutions of government for our safety and happiness, and particularly the national one now lately instituted; for the civil and religious liberty with which we are blessed....

> And also that we may then unite in most humbly offering our prayers and supplications to the great Lord and Ruler of Nations, and beseech Him to pardon our national and other transgressions, to enable us all, whether in public or private stations, to perform our several and relative duties properly and punctually, to render our national government a blessing to all the People, by constantly being a government of wise, just and constitutional laws, discreetly and faithfully executed and obeyed, to protect and guide all Sovereigns and Nations (especially such as have shown kindness unto us) and to bless them with good government, peace, and concord, to promote the knowledge and practice of the true religion and virtue, and the increase of science among them and us, and generally to grant unto all Mankind such a degree of temporal prosperity as He alone knows to be best.

This fervent proclamation indicates quite clearly where the hearts of the American people turned to for their blessings. Today, our school children think that the Pilgrims thanked the Indians, not God, on Thanksgiving Day. Our children are being lied to by our educators, and what good can come from such lies?

One merely has to read the prayers that Washington wrote in his own personal prayer book to understand how deeply he was imbued with the Holy Spirit and how deeply he relied on God for all matters of importance in his life. And it is this aspect of Washington's character that is rarely if ever referred to in school textbooks. Even so great a man as Washington could fall to his knees and pray for forgiveness. In one prayer, he wrote:

> I have sinned and done very wickedly, be merciful to me, O God, and pardon me for Jesus Christ's sake.... Thou gavest Thy Son to die for me; and has given me assurance of salvation, upon my repentance and sincerely endeavoring to conform my life to His holy precepts and example.

We must forever praise God and thank Him for raising up such a leader as George Washington, the father of our country. Isn't it a tragedy that American children are no longer taught about this tower of a man who should be their hero? I remember when I was in first grade, there was a portrait of George Washington in our classroom. That portrait looked down upon us children and I revered him. It was the Stuart portrait, in which the bottom part was unfinished. But to me it looked as if George Washington were in heaven.

Americans revered George Washington with good reason. But today he is just a figure on a one-dollar bill.

Noah Webster

Another great American whose godly influence was felt by millions of children was Noah Webster, whose blue-backed speller taught millions to read and spell. In 1828, Webster completed his *American Dictionary of the English Language.* In this dictionary are constant references to God and the Bible, for Webster was an orthodox Christian. He stated:

> Education is useless without the Bible. God's Word, contained in the Bible, has furnished all necessary rules to direct our conduct.

He also wrote:

> In my view, the Christian religion is the most important and one of the first things in which all children, under a free government ought to be instructed. ... No truth is more evident to my mind than that the Christian religion must be the basis of any government intended to secure the rights and privileges of a free people.

Alexis de Tocqueville

This strong American adherence to Biblical religion impressed the French historian Alexis de Tocqueville who traveled throughout America in the early 1830s and wrote a marvelous book about his observations. He wrote:

> In the United States the sovereign authority is religious.... [T]here is no country in the world where the Christian religion retains a greater influence over the souls of men than in America, and there can be no greater proof of its utility and of its conformity to human nature than that its influence is powerfully felt over the most enlightened and free nation of the earth....
>
> America is great because America is good, and if America ever ceases to be good, America will cease to be great.
>
> The safeguard of morality is religion, and morality is the best security of law as well as the surest pledge of freedom.
>
> The Americans combine the notions of Christianity and of liberty so intimately in their minds, that it is impossible to make them conceive the one without the other.

Abraham Lincoln

It is hard for us to believe that thirty years later this Christian nation would be torn asunder and plunged into a civil war that took a half million American lives. Men prayed to the same God on both sides of the conflict. In his second inaugural address after the defeat of the Confederacy, Lincoln said:

> The prayers of both [sides] could not be answered. That of neither has been answered fully. The Almighty has His own purposes. "Woe unto the world because of offenses; for it must needs be that offenses come, but woe to that man by whom the offense cometh."

And then Lincoln concluded with these famous words:

> With malice toward none, with charity for all, with firmness in the right, as God gives us to see the right, let us strive on to finish the work we are in, to bind up the nation's wounds, to care for him who shall have borne the battle, and for his widow, and his orphan — to do all which may achieve and cherish a just and lasting peace among ourselves and with all nations.

Indeed, only Christian charity could restore the United States as one nation, under God, with liberty and justice for all.

America's Christian heritage is so rich, so powerful, so sustaining, that even President Clinton felt compelled to end his second inaugural address, stating:

> May God strengthen our hands for the good work ahead, and always, always bless our America.

How sincere was the President, we have no way to know. We know his faults, we know his immorality. Yet, even the profoundly sinful must face the consequences of his sins. Obviously, President Clinton, born in the Southern Bible Belt, must reflect his Baptist roots if he is to maintain a modicum of credibility among his fellow Southerners.

Our secular education system, of course, makes the teaching of Biblical religion to American children impossible, but nothing prevents our educators from inculcating the moral principles of humanism which emphatically teach that there is no connection between religion and morality. Moral relativism, situational ethics, sexual freedom, and multiculturalism, which teaches that all values systems are equally valid, are now the order of the day.

Chuck Colson, the former special counsel to President Nixon who went to prison for his role in the Watergate cover-up, underwent a religious conversion that changed his life. In 1993, he lectured on the subject, "Can We Be Good Without God?" He said:

> What we fail to realize is that rejecting transcendental truth is tantamount of committing national suicide. A secular state cannot cultivate virtue.... We are taking away the spiritual element and abandoning morality based on religious truth, counting instead on our heads and our subjective feeling to make us do what is right.

And that is exactly what our educators are doing when they talk about universal values, basic values, and common values as if 3,000 years of Judeo-Christian values are totally irrelevant or never existed.

At the age of fifteen, George Washington copied in his own handwriting 110 "Rules of Civility and Decent Behavior in Company and Conversation." Rule 108 stated:

> When you speak of God, or His attributes, let it be seriously and with reverence. Honor and obey your natural parents although they be poor.

How about distributing that book among American school children! Abigail Adams wrote to her son Quincy Adams in 1780:

> The only sure and permanent foundation of virtue is religion. Let this important truth be engraved upon your heart.... Justice, humanity and benevolence are the duties you owe to society in general. To your country the same duties are incumbent upon you with the additional obligation of sacrificing ease, pleasure, wealth and life itself for its defense and security.

Thus was the American character formed in the early days of the republic. Which means that as long as we continue to maintain a secular government education system, we shall be plagued with all of the social problems that are the natural results of secular morality.

How long will it take for Americans to abandon our godless education system? It won't happen until Christian leaders exhort Christian parents to leave these schools. When will this happen? Perhaps never.

The average Christian "leader" is anything but a leader. Meanwhile, parents are slowly but surely making their own decisions about their children's education without the help of politically correct Christian leadership. And that is why the homeschool and Christian school movement continues to grow exponentially. It's the only proper decision for Christian parents to make in New Age America.

God the Educator

If we want to understand what God had in mind when He created man, all we have to do is read Genesis 1:26-28 in the King James version of the Bible:

> And God said, Let us make man in our image, after our likeness: and let them have dominion over the fish of the sea, and over the fowl of the air, and over the cattle, and over all the earth, and over every creeping thing that creepeth upon the earth. So God created man in his own image, in the image of God created he him; male and female created he them. And God blessed them, and God said unto them, Be fruitful and multiply, and replenish the earth, and subdue it.

What does this mean? It means that God created man to be like Him, not to be another god, but to be like God, with creative powers and intelligence that no other creature possessed. The ability to have dominion meant that man would be superior to the animal kingdom and be separate and apart from it and be able to make use of it for his benefit. To replenish the earth and subdue it meant that man was to become a farmer, a horticulturist, a conservationist, a gardener. He was to treat the earth as his possession, to nurture it, to care for it, to gain nourishment and wealth from it. He also gave man the power of language, which was not given to any animal. It was the power of language, the power of fine definition that permitted man to take dominion and convert God's raw materials into food, clothing, and shelter.

God then did something quite significant. We read in Genesis 2:19-20:

> And out of the ground the Lord God formed every beast of the field and every fowl of the air, and brought them unto Adam to see what he would call them: and whatsoever Adam called every living creature, that was the name thereof. And Adam gave names to all cattle, and to the fowl of the air, and to every beast of the field.

In other words, God made Adam into an observer of the natural world, a scientist, and a lexicographer — an expander of language, a maker of dictionaries. This was God's first step in educating Adam, to make sure that Adam knew he was not an animal, that he was apart from the animal kingdom, with gifts that permitted him to dominate the animal world. In other words, man was created by God to be a scientist, explorer, inventor, and also husband, father, head of his family, and, as we read in Deuteronomy 6, educator to his children.

And God accomplished all of this by programming Adam's brain so that it would have innate natural faculties, which no animal would have. Thus it is that every child learns to speak his own language virtually from birth, so that by the time he is ready for some kind of formal education, he or she has developed a speaking vocabulary in the thousands of words. The gift of language was the necessary and indispensable instrument for dominion.

Darwin's theories changed all of that. He claimed that human beings were merely higher animals that had evolved from lower animals, and that all of our special faculties were the result of evolutionary accidents and not any special natural gifts from God. B.F. Skinner, the famous behavioral psychologist who developed operant conditioning as a teaching technique, called language "verbal behavior," an evolutionary development from the bark, the chirp, and the meow.

Since the 1930s, progressive educators have worked overtime to reduce American education to animal training. It was Edward L. Thorndike, the eminent educational psychologist at Teachers College, Columbia University, who early in the century formulated the stimuli-and-response "laws" of animal training as they applied to the teaching of children. He wrote, "The best way with children may often be, in the pompous words of an animal trainer, 'to arrange everything in connection with the trick so that the animal will be compelled by the laws of his own nature to perform it.'"

Indeed, it was Thorndike who did more to integrate evolutionary theory into educational practice than anyone else. In the last paragraph of his book, *Animal Intelligence*, published in 1911, he wrote:

> Nowhere more truly than in his mental capacities is man a part of nature. His instincts, that is, his inborn tendencies to feel and act in certain ways, show throughout marks of kinship with the lower animals, especially with our nearest relatives physically, the monkeys. His sense-powers show no new creation. His intellect we have seen to be a simple though extended variation from the general animal sort. This again is presaged by the similar variation in the case of the monkeys. Amongst the minds of animals that of man leads, not as a demigod from another planet, but as a king from the same race.

Telling children that they are animals, part of the animal kingdom, and training them as animals has been the downfall of American education. It is the reason why the Bible cannot be permitted in the public school, because it claims that man was created in God's image, is separate and apart from the animal world, and was instructed by God to take dominion over the animal world.

Today, over four million children in American public schools are required to take the powerful drug Ritalin to make their behavior conform to school demands. Student violence is at an all-time high. Functional illiteracy is rampant among students. Sexual promiscuity is widespread among teenagers, resulting in an epidemic of venereal disease, unwanted pregnancies, abortions. We are producing barbaric children and young adults who do not know how to use their minds because they no longer have them. Their intellects no longer exist. They have been denied God's curriculum, which is so clearly outlined in the Bible by the creative capabilities He gave man.

Is this not a crime? Is it not a crime to take a perfectly healthy, normal human child, train him or her up as an animal, destroy the special intellectual gifts which God gave that human being, so that he or she will live the life of a stunted mental cripple, unable to enjoy a good book, a philosophical conversation, or a sense of what it means to be a child of God? That is why all talk of education reform is just so much hogwash, so much establishment hot air, so much political posturing. For as long as behavioral psychologists control the curriculum, including the content and instruction methods of public education, the schools will never be able to attain the intellectual competence they once were capable of.

How to Teach History to Children

Several months ago, a mother brought her twelve-year-old son, Daniel, to me to be tutored. I had taught the child to read at the age of four with Alpha-Phonics, after which he could read the *New York Times* with ease. He's an intelligent child with great intellectual curiosity. But in public school he is considered a bit of a troublemaker, uncooperative, and a poor student who does sloppy homework. His mother brought him back to me because she wants him to be educated. She had been in constant conflict with Daniel's teachers concerning his intellectual needs, but the school is incapable of providing what she wants. That's why she decided to come back to me.

Since I hadn't seen Daniel in years, I didn't know what his academic deficiencies were. So I began asking him questions. I asked him to name America's wars in chronological order. He couldn't do it. He knew about the American Revolution and the Civil War, but he had no idea when the Civil War took place. In fact, he knew very little U.S. history, and what facts he knew were isolated events that had no connection with one another. His chronological knowledge was zero. In public school he was being taught social studies in which he was learning a lot about Ancient Egypt and how mummies were embalmed.

So I knew what had to be done if Daniel were ever to be educated. He had to be taught history. He had to be taught the proper chronological sequence of events. He had to be taught cause and effect. But how did one start? The reason why the public schools no longer teach history is because they start with evolution and the primordial ooze. Human beings are animals and therefore theoretically have no more history than other animals. Have you ever asked a cat about cat history? Have you ever asked a dog to tell you of the great events in dog history?

But of course, even the evolutionists know that human beings are different from their animal cousins. But being intellectually dishonest, they can claim with a straight face that history has nothing to do with a chronological sequence of events. The notion of history must therefore be perverted so that it illustrates social arrangements on the evolutionary road to socialist utopia. That's what "social" studies are all about. Therefore, children are to be taught about the Eskimos and how they send their elderly grandparents on ice floes to die — a humane sort of euthanasia. Or they are taught about ancient Egypt and the climate that influenced that civilization. Mummification is studied at length because it's spooky and fits in nicely with death education. Why would you want to teach a child about a dry piece of parchment called the U.S.

Constitution? What good would that do, if life is essentially meaningless and traditional history has no social value?

When William Spady, the tireless promoter of Outcome-Based Education, was asked if history was going to be taught in OBE, he said that there should not be a separate course called history "that starts at some ancient time and moves forward to the present." The students should "thoroughly examine current problems, issues, and phenomena in depth and ask why, why, why, about their origins and relationships." But how will the students be able to get an answer to their "whys" unless they know history? Easy. They will use psychology to analyze why something happened. Current problems will be understood in terms of behavioral psychology — with a little Freudian psychoanalysis thrown in to spice things up. And their solutions will also be spelled out in terms of psychology.

But if you believe that man was created by God, in His image, then you require an approach to history that takes that into account. And so, when Daniel came for his first session, we started by reading Genesis and discussing what God had in mind when He created the universe and man. Daniel had never read the Bible before, and therefore it was a revelation to him. It was important for him to know that there was a Creator with the power to create the universe, to create the earth, and to create man. We read that God gave man dominion over the natural world, and we discussed the difference between this understanding of man's responsibility as a steward of the natural world, and the environmentalist view that man is a polluter of the natural world.

We then read how God brought the animals "after their kind" before Adam and told him to name them. What did this mean? It meant that God had made man into a scientist, an objective observer of the natural world, and a lexicographer, an inventor of names and words. God had given man the power of speech, but it was up to man to create his language.

Daniel liked the word "lexicographer" and had to repeat it twice before pronouncing it correctly. I began to realize that the Bible should really be the first book in history, if one is to teach history as the story of man on earth and his relationship with his Creator. It is that relationship that not only gives meaning to one's life, but gives meaning to history itself.

We then read further into Genesis, God's creation of Eve, the temptation of Eve by the serpent in the Garden of Eden, the eating of the forbidden fruit, and its consequences, not only for Adam and Eve, but for all mankind. In God's words, "In sorrow shalt thou eat of it all the days of thy life." That's powerful stuff. But if you want to instill a deep sense of morality in a child, is there a better way to do it? Is it too difficult for a twelve-year-old to understand the reason for man's fall — disobedience to God — and realize that he will be morally tested every day of his life? The old primers used to teach, "In Adam's fall, we sinned all." That was the source of early America's moral backbone.

Deuteronomy tells us that that is what we must teach our children, if they are to begin to understand the power and goodness of God and why they must obey His commandments. And is not history the story of man's struggle with good and evil and of his long sorrowful trail of disobedience?

How much of the Bible should be read before getting into historical narrative? That's a subject for any parent or educator to deal with. My plan, at present, is to have Daniel read well into the Bible, covering the major stories, before getting into traditional history. Over the years, I have collected a number of old history textbooks written at a time when historians believed in God. They are the books that educated early generations of Americans, and they are the ones we shall use. They are limited, of course, in that they usually end before the Civil War. We then shall have to find historians who have written books taking us at least to the turn of the last century. Ridpath comes to mind as a good historian with a readable, dramatic narrative style. Robert Welch, at the age of seven, read all nine huge volumes of Ridpath's *History of the World,* which kindled his lifelong love of history.

I have no idea how long Daniel's mother will want me to tutor him. He may go off to a private school away from home. But this business of teaching history to children is one that is very much worth thinking about.

Recently I had dinner at a friend's house and was chatting with his twelve-year-old daughter who attends a local public school. I asked her how she was doing, and she told me that she hated school — not merely disliked school, but hated it. I had hoped that her parents would homeschool her. But they just couldn't do it. I told her I thought I knew why she hated school — because it was boring. Yes, she replied. It was boring. I thought, education without God is inevitably boring.

And then I said, "And you're probably not learning much also." She wanted to know what I meant by that. So I asked her to name the first three wars that the United States was involved with. She got the first one all right, the Revolutionary War. But the only other war she could think of was the Civil War, and, like Daniel, she had no idea when that took place.

The second war, I told her, was the one fought against the Barbary pirates of North Africa who kidnapped Americans for ransom. An American invasion of Tripolitania brought that war to a victorious end. My friend's daughter had never heard of that war. The fact is that most Americans have never heard of it. But the anthem of the U.S. Marine Corps should remind us: "From the halls of Montezuma, to the Shores of Tripoli…."

The third war was the War of 1812. She had never heard of that one either. She had never heard of the Battle of New Orleans, or the burning of Washington by the British, or Andrew Jackson, the hero of that war who later became our seventh President.

"But I know all about the Industrial Revolution," she volunteered. It turned out that her class had been studying the cotton mills of New England and how young girls were being exploited by the mill owners who were rich and mean. So, at the age of twelve, she was already being indoctrinated to believe that the Industrial Revolution consisted mainly of factory owners exploiting poor young girls.

She had heard of Eli Whitney and the cotton gin. But she had never heard of Robert Fulton and the steamboat. In other words, the public schools were teaching "social studies," not history. Their aim was to indoctrinate children in a pro-socialist view of our history by emphasizing the meanness of capitalism.

I have no doubt that this young girl will go through life associating the Industrial Revolution with those poor girls working in the mills. She accepted the views of her teacher as truth, and they are imbedded in her head unless somewhere down the road of life she realizes that she was indoctrinated by a pro-socialist teacher — as many conservatives learn when they get rid of the socialist notions their public schools inflicted on them.

What kind of nation are we going to have with its best "educated" people devoid of any sense of history? The educators can't solve the reading problem. But they don't even believe that there's a history problem. History as a subject in the public schools has simply been destroyed, and nations that destroy their history end up destroying themselves.

Perhaps the best way to judge a school curriculum is by the way it treats history. In the federal education reform plan known as School-to-Work, we know that the purpose of the curriculum is to create young adults willing to serve the state and the industries that will hire them. Obviously, a knowledge of history is unnecessary in a such a curriculum in which students are supposed to demonstrate their skills as potential members of the workforce. American history is simply irrelevant to what will be taught in School-to-Work.

As for immigrant children who, at one time, studied American history so that they could become Americans, they will be trained to become the willing workers of tomorrow, without a knowledge of our national history, but with lots of social information about slavery, racism, feminism, homophobia, abortion rights, social injustice, economic injustice, injustice toward native Americans, and whatever else the socialists can pour into "social studies." Some of these immigrants, with an undefined but palpable love of America, may eventually discover American history for themselves.

But all is not lost. Many young adults discover history for themselves by reading popular books about historical events or watching the History Channel. There are also thousands of biographies, autobiographies, and memoirs that have been written over the centuries that provide important keys to history. Our publishing houses are bringing out new ones all the time.

Then we have the 1997 publication of Paul Johnson's monumental *History of the American People,* an extraordinary book. Its opening lines create a great sense of anticipation: "The creation of the United States of America is the greatest of all human adventures. No other national story holds such tremendous lessons, for the American people themselves and for the rest of mankind." So, despite "social studies" with all of its perversions of the truth, the idea of history is anything but dead. But what percentage of the children coming out of our public schools will ever discover that, particularly those who can't read or won't read?

As one would expect, homeschoolers are very much interested in history. All you have to do is look at the books being sold at homeschool conventions to realize that history is one of the most popular subjects among them. And since most homeschoolers are Christian, their keen sense of history comes from their study of the Bible, the greatest history book of them all.

Modern technology has also given us some very effective new tools to bring history to anyone who owns a tape player. Reverend J. Steven Wilkins' excellent sixteen-cassette-tape history, *America: The First 350 Years,* can be listened to in one's car or at home while doing chores. Reverend Rushdoony's eighteen-tape cassette course, *American History to 1865,* not only provides the student with an insightful and engrossing view of our early history narrated by one of the great theologians of the twentieth century, but provides a philosophical foundation for understanding what is happening today.

In other words, even those who can't read or have no time to read can learn history by listening to historians tell it in their own words. Thus, the tutor has the additional valuable tools of cassette tapes made by learned Christian scholars to teach children history. Since families do a lot of automobile travelling these days, rather than have the children play electronic games in the back seat, let them listen to tapes narrating the great historical dramas of the past.

Without history, we are indeed like the cats and the dogs. The story of human existence is the story of human experience, from which there is much to learn. To that effect, George Santayana summed up the problem very nicely when he said: "Those who cannot remember the past are condemned to repeat it." Or as Konrad Adenauer put it: "History is the sum total of the things that could have been avoided."

Eugenics and the Christian Ethic

The father of eugenics is generally acknowledged to be Thomas Robert Malthus (1766-1834), the British clergyman and economist who argued in his famous "Essay on the Principle of Population," published in 1798, that the "power of population is indefinitely greater than the power in the earth to produce subsistence for man." He wrote:

> Population, when unchecked, increases in a geometrical ratio. Subsistence increases only in an arithmetical ratio.... By that law of our nature which makes food necessary to the life of man, the effects of these two unequal powers must be kept equal. This implies a strong and constantly operating check on population from the difficulty of subsistence. This difficulty must fall somewhere and must necessarily be severely felt by a large portion of mankind.

In other words, because human population grows so much faster than food production, widespread starvation is inevitable. Malthus believed that this imbalance between food supply and human births was a permanent manifestation of natural law. Somehow, it never occurred to him that food production could be increased dramatically if scientific and mechanical methods were applied to it.

But that is typical of how eugenicists think. Even today we have people like the hysterical Paul Erhlich writing and talking about the population bomb, urging women to stop having children that are polluting the world. Then there are organizations like Zero Population Growth and Negative Population Growth obsessed with overpopulation. The motto of Negative Population Growth is "Fewer People for a Better World." They repeat the Malthusian error by asking the same question that Malthus asked: "How can we put an end to mass starvation and suffering in this world? There is only one answer." The same answer that Malthus gave: fewer people. But there is a much better answer: economic freedom.

In Cuba, food is rationed and people live at a subsistence level because of a communist government. Cuba is one of the world's most fertile countries. But its form of government prevents Cubans from making the most of their own fertile land. Moreover, Cuba is hardly overpopulated. Since the imposition of communism, over a million Cubans have left the island. So, fewer people is hardly the answer to mass starvation.

The long-range goal of Negative Population Growth is to stabilize our U.S. population "at no more than 150 million, and world population at no more than two billion, after an interim period of gradual population decrease." They forget that when we had only 130 million Americans, we also had a depression, with soup kitchens to feed the hungry. Now we have a population of 250 million with so much food that dieting has become a national obsession. Getting rid of 100 million Americans will not make the air cleaner, the water purer, or garbage disposal easier.

It should not surprise Christians that the leading advocates of population control are anti-Christian humanists. Indeed, the Humanist Manifesto 2000 states:

> Large sectors of the world population still do not enjoy the fruits of affluence; they continue to languish in poverty, hunger, and disease, particularly in the developing world.... In 1900 the world had an estimated 1.7 billion people. By the year 2000 it will exceed 6 billion.... If population continues to grow as projected, it will lead to a drastic decrease in available tillable grain lands, which may by 2050 shrink to one-quarter of an acre per person in many countries.... National governments and corporate leaders must abandon short-term policies and support forward-looking planning.

And so, the theories of Malthus are alive and well in the twenty-first century. Apparently, pseudo-scientists have very short memories and tend to ignore those facts that disprove their views. Some of the world's most densely populated countries, such as the Netherlands or Israel, are very well fed. They grow lots of food on less and less acreage, using the most scientifically advanced methods available. But, believe it or not, because of the sharp drop in the fertility rate in Western Europe, Japan, Russia, and elsewhere, demographers see a population decline, not a population explosion in the next fifty years.

Racist Eugenics

After Malthus came Sir Francis Galton (1822-1911), the British pseudo-scientist who studied methods of improving the mental and physical traits of human populations by selective mating. He called this pseudo-science of race, eugenics, from the Greek *eugenes* meaning "well born." He defined eugenics as "the study of the agencies under social control which may improve or impair the racial qualities of future generations physically or mentally."

In 1884, Galton established his Anthropometric Laboratory. He, too, was alarmed at the prolific birthrate of the "less suitable races" and the low birthrate of the "more suitable races." Something had to be done about it. He argued that since mental and physical attributes were inherited, superior human beings should be encouraged to have lots of children, and measures should be taken to lower the birthrate of the lower classes. He was a cousin of Charles Darwin whose idea of the survival of the fittest agreed very well with the new science of eugenics.

In Germany, it was biologist Ernst Haeckel who brought Darwinism into German intellectual life. He saw social Darwinism as a natural force, and he combined a mystical belief in that natural force with the concept of natural selection, which he applied to the social and political arena, with the result that he became one of Germany's leading ideologists for racism, nationalism and imperialism.

In 1895, the German Social Darwinist Alfred Ploetz invented a concept, which he called racial hygiene.

He accused the medical profession of endangering the race by helping individuals who would not have otherwise survived live and reproduce themselves. Social Darwinists in Britain spoke of certain diseases as "our racial friends" because they attacked those with a weak constitution. In 1905, Ploetz founded a Society for Racial Hygiene. In 1907, the word *international* was added to its name. In 1910, Sweden's Society for Racial Hygiene became its first foreign affiliate.

In 1908, Galton founded the Eugenics Society of Great Britain, and in 1912 an international congress on eugenics was convened in London. In 1907, Indiana passed the first laws allowing sterilization of the mentally ill and criminally insane. By the late 1920s similar laws had been passed in twenty-eight states, sanctioned by a 1927 U.S. Supreme Court ruling in *Buck v. Bell*, which held that it was constitutional to involuntarily sterilize the developmentally disabled, the insane, or uncontrollably epileptic. Oliver Wendell Holmes, supported by Louis Brandeis and six other justices, wrote the opinion. As a result, by 1930, 15,000 individuals were sterilized in the United States.

Galton also had a very profound influence on American progressive educators, those members of the Protestant academic elite who no longer believed in the religion of their fathers. They put their new faith in science, evolution, and psychology. Science explained the nature of the material world, evolution explained the origin of living matter, and psychology permitted man to investigate human behavior and develop the means to control it. Thus, the progressives found Galton's scientific racism to be very compatible with their strong belief in evolution and behavioral psychology.

Racist Liberals

James McKeen Cattell, father of modern educational psychology, considered Galton to be "the greatest man I have ever known." In fact, Cattell developed mental tests based on Galton's pioneering efforts to devise the means of measuring racial superiority. One such test was developed and conducted in 1895 by an American, R. Meade Bache. His "Reaction Time with Reference to Race" used an "electro-magnetic physiological apparatus."

Bache tested three groups of males: Caucasians, American Indians, and American Negroes. They were tested for the speed with which they reacted to several items.

The results showed the Indians to have the fastest reaction times, and the Caucasians the slowest. The blacks fell between the two other groups. How did Bache interpret the results? He wrote:

> Pride of race obscures the view of the white with reference to the relative automatic quickness of the negro. That the negro is, in the truest sense, a race inferior to that of the white can be proved by many facts, and among these by the quickness of his automatic movements as compared with those of the white.

In other words, quicker physical reactions are sure signs of racial inferiority! That's pseudo-science showing its true racist bias. And this is the kind of pseudo-science that was used by the progressives to construct a curriculum for the public schools in which the Negro child was relegated to an education befitting his inferior status.

Edward L. Thorndike, Cattell's famous protégé, also adopted Galton's views on inherited intelligence. As a true believer in race science and evolution, he believed that man was an animal that could be trained as an animal. Thus, he invented the stimulus-response technique of behavioral education. He wrote in 1911:

> Nowhere more truly than in his mental capacities is man a part of nature. His instincts, that is, his inborn tendencies to feel and act in certain ways, show throughout marks of kinship with the lower animals, especially with our nearest relatives physically, the monkeys. His sense-powers show no new creation. His intellect we have seen to be a simple though extended variation from the general animal sort. This again is presaged by the similar variation in the case of the monkeys. Amongst the minds of animals that of man leads, not as a demigod from another planet, but as a king from the same race.

Thus, the idea that man was made in God's image went out the school window. Both Cattell and Thorndike had fathers who were Christian ministers. So they knew the Bible very well. Their apostasy destroyed American education. Thus, with America's top educators adapting the ideas of eugenics to the problems of education, eugenics as scientific racism acquired widespread respectability. It should also be noted that the I.Q. test was a direct result of the eugenics enterprise, serving as a means of sifting out the mentally superior.

Racist Feminists

One of the individuals attracted to the new science was a woman by the name of Margaret Sanger (1879-1966). In 1910, she, her husband, and three children moved to New York City where she became immersed in the radical bohemian culture of Greenwich Village. She and her husband joined a circle of left-wing, communist, and anarchist intellectuals that included Max Eastman, John Reed, Upton Sinclair, Mabel Dodge, and Emma Goldman. She also joined the Women's Committee of the New York Socialist Party.

Sanger's work as a visiting nurse turned her interest to sex education and women's health. Influenced by anarchist Emma Goldman, she began to advocate the need for family limitation as a means by which working-class women could liberate themselves from the burden of unwanted pregnancy. In 1914, Sanger published the first issue of *The Woman Rebel*, which advocated militant feminism and the right to practice birth control. She also wrote a sixteen-page pamphlet, *Family Limitation*, which provided explicit instructions on the use of contraceptive methods. In August 1914, Sanger was indicted for violating postal obscenity laws. She jumped bail in October and set sail for England.

In England she contacted a number of British radicals, feminists, and neo-Malthusians whose social and economic theories helped her develop broader scientific and social justifications for birth control. She was also deeply influenced by psychologist Havelock Ellis and his theories on female sexuality and free love. Separated from her husband in 1914, Sanger embarked on a series of affairs with several men, including Havelock Ellis and H.G. Wells.

In 1915, Sanger returned to the United States. The government's case against her was dropped, so she embarked on a nationwide tour to drum up publicity. In 1916, she opened the nation's first birth control clinic in Brooklyn, New York. After nine days of operation, the clinic was raided, and Sanger and staff were arrested. She spent thirty days in jail. However, the publicity surrounding the clinic provided Sanger with a base of wealthy supporters from which she began to build an organized birth control movement.

In 1917, Sanger published a new monthly, the *Birth Control Review*, and in 1921 she embarked on a campaign to win mainstream support for birth control by founding the American Birth Control League, the forerunner of Planned Parenthood. She focused her efforts on gaining support from the medical profession, social workers, and the liberal wing of the eugenics movement. Havelock Ellis had converted her to the eugenics creed. She saw birth control as a means of reducing genetically transmitted mental or physical defects, and supported sterilization for the mentally incompetent. She advocated "more children for the fit, less from the unfit that is the chief issue of birth control."

In 1922, Sanger married oil magnate James Noah H. Slee, thus insuring her financial independence. Slee, who died in 1943, became the main funder of the birth control movement. By connecting with the eugenicsmovement, Sanger was able to gain the backing of some of America's wealthiest people.

In 1921, the Second International Congress of Eugenics was convened at New York's American Museum of Natural History under President Henry Fairfield Osborn. While Major Leonard Darwin, son of Charles Darwin, had been president of the First Congress of Eugenics in 1912, none other than Winston Churchill had been its vice-president. The Second Congress drew an equally impressive number of attendees: Herbert Hoover, soon-to-be President of the U.S., Gifford Pinchot, future governor of Pennsylvania, Robert M. Yerkes, chief psychologist of the U.S. Army, and Edward L. Thorndike, chairman of the psychology department at Teachers College. The principal benefactress of the Congress was Mrs. E.H. Harriman, wife of the railroad magnate and mother of Averell Harriman. The Congress was dedicated to saving America by increasing the fecundity of its best breeding stock. The complaint was that the New England stock was not holding its own.

Immigration from Eastern and Southern Europe was seen as the great threat to WASP dominance and therefore had to be curtailed. At the close of the Eugenics Congress, the exhibits were transferred to the U.S. Capitol in Washington, where Congressmen could ponder the terrible effects that unbridled immigration was having on America's Anglo-Saxon and Northern European genetic pool.

Much "research" had gone into creating these exhibits. In 1904, Harvard Ph.D. Charles Benedict Davenport (1866-1944), a leading eugenicist, set up his Laboratory of Experimental Evolution at Cold Spring Harbor, Long Island, New York, with help from the Carnegie Endowment. He established a Eugenics Record Office financed by Mrs. Harriman. Davenport promoted the idea of Aristogenics, the selection and mating of individuals with superior blood to produce a new American race of Super-Nordics. Years later, Marxist Hermann J. Muller would advocate collecting sperm from a few outstanding males to be used in artificial insemination, producing large numbers of superior offspring sired by the same man.

Davenport's publications had a profound effect on the U.S. House of Representatives Committee on Immigration and Naturalization, which finally got Congress to enact its Immigration Act of 1924. The Act severely limited immigration from Southern and Eastern Europe. This was quite a victory for the eugenics movement.

In 1930, Sanger opened a family planning clinic in Harlem with the approval of the Negro leadership, including communist W.E.B. DuBois. Beginning in 1939, DuBois also served on the advisory council for Sanger's "Negro Project." The financial support of Albert and Mary Lasker made the project possible. In 1966, the year Sanger died, the Rev. Martin Luther King, Jr., said, "There is a striking kinship between our movement and Margaret Sanger's early efforts."

In 1930, Pope Pius XI condemned eugenics in his encyclical *Casti connubii*. In 1933, Germany passed its own sterilization law. The Nazis simply changedthe voluntary one proposed by the Weimar Republic to one that permitted compulsory sterilization. From 1934 to 1937, an estimated 400,000 sterilizations took place in Germany. In the United States, about 30,000 had been sterilized on eugenics grounds by 1939.

In October 1939, Hitler began a euthanasia program. He secretly authorized doctors to grant a merciful death to patients judged to be incurably ill. A key justification for this was to be found in the book, *Release and Destruction of Lives Not Worth Living* (1920) by Alfred Hoche, a professor of medicine, and Rudolf Binding, a professor of law.

In 1935, British physicians founded a Euthanasia Legalization Society, which submitted a bill to allow voluntary euthanasia. However, the British were not quite ready for that. Meanwhile, the war with its racist horrors gave eugenics and racism a bad name. So the American Eugenics Society became the Society for the Study of Social Biology. In 1950, the American Society of Human Genetics was established and, in 1954, the American Journal of Human Genetics.

Abortion

From the end of World War II to the present, Planned Parenthood has become the world's largest and most powerful enterprise promoting birth control and abortion. It was greatly helped by two U.S. Supreme Court decisions: *Griswold v. Connecticut* in

1965, which legalized birth control among married couples, and *Roe v. Wade* in 1973, which legalized abortion nationwide.

Legalized abortion became the slippery slope leading to fetal tissue experimentation. Actually, fetal tissue transplantation in a patient had been tried as early as 1928. Now, it is routinely done privately. Planned Parenthood states:

> A woman's choice to donate to medical research a fetus she has aborted begins and ends with her.... Knowing she can donate her aborted fetus to potentially lifesaving medical research may help a woman turn an unintended pregnancy of which she may feel a sense of loss into a social good.

In 1998, nearly five million individuals, including teenagers, received some kind of "reproductive health services" at Planned Parenthood. This includes 167,928 abortions performed in the organization's 850 clinics. In 1998, 1,333 affiliate staff and volunteer educators provided 100,000 educational programs — from preschool to universities.

Meanwhile, the free love that Margaret Sanger enjoyed as a socialist bohemian has become the recreational sex movement of the New Age. It has had a devastating effect on the health of young Americans. According to Planned Parenthood, at least sixty-five million people, more than one in five Americans, are believed to be infected with a viral STI other than HIV. They include genital herpes, human papilloma virus, and hepatitis B. In

1996 there were an estimated three million new cases of chlamydia making it the most prevalent bacterial STI in the United States.

The Loss of Christian Culture

When one surveys the history of the eugenics and birth control movements, one must conclude that never has Christian civilization sustained a more relentless and devastating assault on its principles and values. Humanism, socialism, communism, statism, nourished by the theory of evolution and its atheist implications, have reduced Christianity to fighting a defensive rear action campaign to maintain its influence in American culture. Although a large majority of Americans claim to believe in God, religion has become relegated to a few hours of Sunday church service and periodic observance of traditional holidays, which have become more and more secularized over the years.

Andrew Sandlin has summed it up very nicely. He writes: "What is termed the 'culture wars' really constitutes religious wars fought on cultural battlegrounds. It is a conflict of religious visions.... Secularism could obtain cultural hegemony only by marginalizing another establishment of religion, Christianity. Culture wars are really just the wide, public manifestations of religious wars over what the character of society should be."

And so, the secular juggernaut in the form of eugenics, birth control, and population control all bear on how we regard human life and human origins. If we are products of the primordial ooze, then we have no rights other than those our betters confer on us. But if we are made in the image of God, then our rights are inalienable, endowed by the Living God, and governments are made by men to secure these rights. Christians have no choice but to resist what is contrary to God's law as given us in Holy Scripture. If we don't, then we give up the security of our God-given rights.

Today, Americans live lives of extreme contradiction. We want both the blessings of God and the pleasures and conveniences of secularism. Like open marriages, we want the security of marital fidelity and the pleasures of extramarital relations. We want the love of children and the right to kill them in the womb. We want to be both virtuous and sinful, obedient and disobedient, good and bad. And that is why so many Americans today are in some form of psychotherapy, or taking some kind of mood altering drug. The gnawing guilt that comes from sinful behavior cannot be wished away. Many now come to Christ in the hope that their sins can be washed away in the blood of the cross. The burden of guilt has become too heavy.

But that is also why so many Americans turn to atheism and humanism. They prefer to deceive themselves rather than admit of the existence of God. That is why they are perfectly willing to believe in the theory of evolution, even though the complexity of genetic organization makes godless evolution an impossibility. Intellectual pride can make self-deception a very satisfactory way of life by simply distorting reality.

So where are we headed? The Christian remnant, as small as it is, grows in strength every day through the quality of the individuals and families that become part of it.

Biblical religion is making its comeback because of the moral blind alley that secularism is leading us into. The unrelenting attacks on religion, like the unrelenting attacks on the Second Amendment, are stirring up resistance among those thoughtful enough to recognize the dangers to freedom inherent in these attacks. The idealism of the progressives has been replaced by the cynicism of the establishment. What made the eugenics movement acceptable in the early part of the twentieth century was destroyed in World War II.

There is more reason to be hopeful about the future than there has been in years. More people are studying the Bible than ever before simply because modern philosophy has led humanity into an intolerable dead end. So we return to the Bible because it endures, because its wisdom is timeless, because God's Word will prevail above the din, today, tomorrow, and forever.

Is Humanism a Religion?

The question is important. For humanism is the worldview of our educational leaders, of the textbooks they write, of the psychologists who counsel our youngsters on values, sex and death. In short, it is the worldview of the curricula used in the public schools. In fact, humanism forms the philosophical basis of what passes for teacher education in our state colleges and universities.

Establishments of Religion

Thus, if humanism is indeed a religion, then what we have in our public schools and state colleges and universities are government-supported establishments of religion, which are patently unconstitutional and therefore illegal.

In fact, it should be pointed out that on March 4, 1987, U.S. District Judge W. Brevard Hand, in *Smith v. Board of School Commissioners of Mobile County, Alabama*, ruled that secular humanism is a religion. The 172-page ruling defines religion and concludes, after reviewing the relevant aspects of humanism, that "For purposes of the First Amendment, secular humanism is a religious belief system, entitled to the protections of, and subject to the prohibitions of, the religion clauses."

Three Key Documents

Judge Hand wrote:

> The entire body of thought has three key documents that furnish the text upon which the belief system rests as a platform: *Humanist Manifesto I*, *Humanist Manifesto II*, and the *Secular Humanist Declaration*.
>
> These factors...demonstrate the *institutional* character of secular humanism. They are evidence that this belief system is similar to groups traditionally afforded protection by the First Amendment religion clauses.

The judge then went on to demonstrate that forty-four textbooks being used in the public schools of Alabama were written from the humanist point of view and thereby constituted an illegal establishment of religion. The judge ordered the books removed from the schools.

On August 26, 1987, the Eleventh Circuit Court reversed Judge Hand's order banning the forty-four textbooks. The higher court did not address the question of whether secular humanism is a religion for First Amendment purposes, but asserted that it was not being promoted in the textbooks that were banned.

Judge Frank M. Johnson Jr. wrote:

> Use of the challenged textbooks has the primary effect of conveying information that is essentially neutral in its religious content to the school children who utilize the books; none of these books convey a message of government approval of secular humanism....
>
> There simply is nothing in the record to indicate that omission of certain facts regarding religion from these textbooks of itself constituted an advancement of secular humanism or an active hostility towards theistic religion.

And so the books were put back in the schools.

The Wrong Question

But the question is not whether the textbooks are humanistic or not, but whether the entire government education system is an establishment of the humanist religion. All of the rationales used to remove Bibles and other indications and manifestations of the Judeo-Christian theistic worldview from classrooms are based on the First Amendment's prohibition against government establishments of religion.

But if it can be shown that the entire government system of education — from the elementary schools to the state colleges and universities — are establishments of the humanist religion, the courts would have no choice but to order the closing down of these institutions.

There can be no government establishment of religion in the United States.

From Nonsectarianism to Secularism

When the public schools were first established, the courts ruled that the schools had to be nonsectarian, that is, not favoring any particular Protestant denomination. That they were essentially Protestant in character was generally acknowledged. In fact, the reason why Catholics established their own parochial school system was because they recognized the Protestant character of the public schools.

After the turn of the century, however, as humanist progressives took control of the government schools, nonsectarianism gradually gave way to secularism. Secularists hold that any government institution that promotes or supports belief in the existence of a supernatural being is an establishment of religion.

As more and more judges adopted the secularist point of view, order after order was handed down stripping the public schools of the vestiges of nonsectarian Christianity. Curricula were revised, new textbooks written, new programs instituted so that today's public schools not only no longer reflect the nation's Judeo-Christian heritage but now constitute the most powerful educational machine for the propagation of humanism among the American people.

Filling the Vacuum

The secularists had no intention of creating a neutral, nontheistic vacuum in our schools. Their plan always was to get rid of Judeo-Christian values and replace them with their own. In this way, the government schools have become, beyond a shadow of a doubt, establishments of the humanist religion.

Today, humanist beliefs are inculcated through such programs and concepts as values clarification, sensitivity training, situational ethics, evolution, multiculturalism, globalism, transcendental meditation, sex education, death education, etc. All of these programs are marbleized throughout the curriculum — in reading, language arts, math, social studies, health education, psychology, art, biology, and other subjects. It is impossible for a student in a government school to avoid or escape the all-pervasive influence of humanist ideas and beliefs which confront and accost him daily every which way he turns.

That the plan of the humanists was to supplant traditional theistic religion with a new man-centered religion of their own can be proven by simply quoting the humanists themselves. The best source of these quotes is *The Humanist* magazine.

The Humanists Organize

The forerunner of *The Humanist* was *The New Humanist* which first appeared in 1928 as a monthly bulletin of the Humanist Fellowship, an organization formed by Unitarian students from the University of Chicago and its related theological schools. Its early editors — Harold Buschman, Edwin H. Wilson, and Raymond B. Bragg — were young Unitarian ministers. It was on the initiatives of Bragg that the drafting of *A Humanist Manifesto*

(1933) was begun. Professor Roy Wood Sellars wrote the first draft. The Manifesto appeared in the April 1933 issue of *The New Humanist*.

The Manifesto was more than just an affirmation of the humanist worldview, it was also a declaration of war against orthodox, traditional religion. The Manifesto's views toward religion can be summed up as follows:

1. The purpose of man's life is "the complete realization of human personality." "[T]he quest for the good life is the…central task for man."

2. The humanist's religious emotions are expressed in "social passion," in a "heightened sense of personal life and in a cooperative effort to promote social well-being."

3. Humanists believe that "all associations and institutions exist for the fulfillment of human life." Therefore, "the intelligent evaluation, transformation, control, and direction of such associations and institutions…is the purpose and program of humanism."

In other words, the humanist must take over society's associations and institutions in order to transform them into instruments of humanist purpose. This includes the institutions of traditional religion.

The Manifesto states: "Certainly religious institutions, their ritualistic forms, ecclesiastical methods, and communal activities must be reconstituted as rapidly as experience allows, in order to function effectively in the modern world."

A Messianic Mission

In other words, the messianic mission of the humanists is not to build new institutions of their own, but to subvert and appropriate the institutions of others. This is not a new idea among humanists. The Unitarians subverted Harvard and took it from its Calvinist founders. Religious liberals have appropriated Yale, Princeton, Dartmouth and other institutions founded by the orthodox.

The loss of these institutions, incidentally, has forced conservative Christians to create new institutions of their own: Bob Jones University, Liberty University, Regent University, Pensacola Christian College, and others. The rise of these new institutions has dismayed the humanists who believed that once the major institutions of traditional religion were subverted and taken over, the influence of theistic religion would fade forever. The hopeful demise of traditional theistic religion is a theme frequently expressed by humanist writers.

Humanism as Religion

Roy Wood Sellars, who drafted *Humanist Manifesto I*, wrote in *The Humanist* (Volume 1, 1941, p. 5) in an article entitled "Humanism as a Religion":

> Undeniably there is something imaginative and daring in bringing together in one phrase two such profoundly symbolic words as humanism and religion. An intimate union is foreshadowed in which religion will become humanistic and humanism religious. And I believe that such a

> synthesis is imperative if humanity is ever to achieve a firm and adequate understanding of itself and its cosmic situation....
>
> To the thoughtful of our day, humanism is being offered as this kind of a religion, a religion akin to science and philosophy and yet not a mere abstract of these specialized endeavors.... Religious humanism rests upon the bedrock of a decision that it is, in the long run, saner and wiser to face facts than to live in a world of fable.

Humanity as God

An article by Oliver L. Reiser, a signer of the Manifesto, in the same issue of *The Humanist*, states:

> The one great hope for democracy lies in the development of a nonsupernaturalistic religion which, unlike other intellectual movements, will be non-academic in its appeal to all civilized individuals. This new foundation for a coming world-order must be the emergent outcome of the thought-content of a universalized culture....
>
> The god of this coming world-religion, that is, the object of reverence of scientific humanism, is the spirit of humanity in its upward striving.

Another signer of the Manifesto, William Floyd, wrote in *The Humanist* (Volume 2, 1942, page 2):

> The religious philosophy of humanism as a substitute for metaphysical theology will enable men to realize the highest value in life without surrendering their minds to any final dogma or any alleged revelation of the supernatural....

> To fill the need for a modern conception of religious foundations the *Humanist Manifesto* was issued in 1933.

Another signer, A. Eustace Haydon, wrote in that same issue:

> Like all religions humanism has its worldview, techniques and ideal.

In Volume VI, p. 6 of *The Humanist* (1946), E. Burdette Backus, a Manifesto signer, wrote:

> [Humanism] is indeed a religion, and the extent to which it is capable of eliciting the emotions of men is limited only by a degree in which those who have made it their own shall succeed in embodying its full riches.

Naturalistic Religion

In an article entitled "Religion Without God" (*The Humanist*, Vol. VII, 1947, p. 9), Kenneth L. Patton wrote:

> A naturalistic religion is just as inclusive of all that is within the world we know as is the supernaturalistic or theistic religion.
>
> Whereas the theist pins his faith and hope in his God, the humanist and naturalist pins his faith in the natural world, and in man as a creature within it, and his faith is no less magnificent, courageous and hopeful than that of the believer in God.

The Fourth Faith

In June 1951 *The Humanist* published an article by Manifesto signer Edwin H. Wilson, entitled "Humanism: The Fourth Faith." He wrote:

> Today, I am suggesting that there is in the world as a present and potent faith, embraced by vast numbers, yet seldom mentioned — a fourth faith namely Humanism. This fourth faith — with rare exceptions such as some Universalist or Unitarian churches, a few independent Humanist Fellowships and the Ethical Societies — has no church to embody it.... Theirs is a secular faith.

According to Wilson, the other three faiths are Protestantism, Catholicism, and Judaism. Since many of the signers of the Manifesto were Unitarians, it is not surprising that Wilson identifies the Unitarian church as belonging to the fourth faith.

In 1952, *The Humanist* (September-October) published an article by Julian Huxley entitled "Evolutionary Humanism: The World's Next Great Religion." Mr. Huxley wrote:

> Out of the needs of our time, through the evolutionary process, a new religion is rising. By religion...I mean an organized system of ideas and emotions which relates man to his destiny, over and above the practical affairs of every day, transcending the present and the existing systems of law and social structure.... I believe we have nothing to lose by using the word "religion" in the broadest sense to include nontheistic formulations and systems as well.

In the next issue of *The Humanist*, Huxley wrote:

> The next phase of history could, and should, be a Humanist phase. Let us help toward its emergence.

Glorification of Man

In an article entitled "The Humanist Faith Today" (*The Humanist*, Vol. 15, No. 4, 1954, p. 180), we read:

> Since humanism appears as a genuinely living option for many people, especially among students, teachers, and intellectuals generally, it may be appropriately studied as a religion. Indeed, it is not unfair to call it the fourth main religious option, along with Judaism, Roman Catholicism, and Protestantism, for thoughtful men in the contemporary Western world....
>
> What remains of religion when the Humanist criticism has completed its work? The Humanist replies that devotion to human and social values emerges as the essence of religion. As [Corliss] Lamont has written, the Humanist postulates that "the chief end of thought and action is to further earthly human interests in behalf of the greater happiness and glory of man."

In 1959, George E. Axtelle, newly elected president of the American Humanist Association, said:

> Ours is no revealed religion. It is a religion, an intellectual and moral outlook shaped by the more sensitive and sympathetic souls of our time.... Ours is a task, not a doctrine.... *Our fundamental goal must be to make the Humanist Way of Life a reality in our communities, our state and our nation.*

The New Religion

In the January-February 1962 issue of *The Humanist*, Sir Julian Huxley wrote an article entitled "The Coming New Religion of Humanism." He wrote:

> The beliefs of this religion of evolutionary humanism are not based on revelation in the supernatural sense, but on the revelations that science and learning have given us about man and the universe. A humanist believes with full assurance that man is not alien to nature, but a part of nature, albeit a unique one.... His true destiny is to guide the future course of evolution on earth towards greater fulfilment, so as to realize more and higher potentialities....
>
> A humanist religion will have the task of redefining the categories of good and evil in terms of fulfilment and of desirable or undesirable realizations of potentiality, and setting up new targets for its morality to aim at....
>
> Humanism also differs from all supernaturalist religions in centering its long-term aims not on the next world but on this.... The humanist goal must therefore be ... the Fulfilment Society.

Secularists Object

Not all humanists agreed with Huxley. Harry Elmer Barnes and Herbert T. Rosenfeld responded with an article of their own in the July-August 1962 issue. They wrote:

> In our opinion, Sir Julian has set forth not the Humanist ideology of today, but a truly noble and eloquent Unitarian sermon. It is Unitarian doctrine, pure if not simple....
>
> It was, of course, frequently argued in earlier decades of our century that Humanism is a secular religion, but in the light of the history of thought and culture, the terms "religion" and "secular" are, in our

> view, mutually exclusive.... If there is any one thing which characterizes and justifies Humanism it is complete and undeviating secularism....
>
> If Humanism is identical with the latter [Unitarianism] in its ideology, we see little basis for a separate Humanist movement or organization.

Edwin H. Wilson, a Unitarian minister and one of the founders of the humanist movement, responded to the Barnes-Rosenfeld article in the Nov.-Dec. 1962 issue. He told of how the magazine was founded by Unitarian theological students. He went on:

> The American Humanist Association itself was organized soon thereafter by a group composed primarily of liberal ministers and professors who were predominantly Unitarians and considered themselves as religious humanists. At the time of its incorporation in 1941, the decision was made not to try to establish humanist churches but to function as an educational movement among humanists wherever they were found.
>
> The early literature of the movement was devoted chiefly to the development of Humanism as a distinctly religious position....
>
> Of the thirty-four persons who signed the *Humanist Manifesto* in 1933, all but four can be readily identified as "religious humanists" who considered Humanism as the development of a better and truer religion and as the next step ahead for those who sought it....
>
> My conviction is that a probe into what is actually believed would show that the "liberal Unitarian

> position" and what is generally presented as Humanism — whether as a religion or as a philosophy — differ very little....
>
> One minister who belongs to the A.H.A. said: "We Unitarians in my church have no ideological conflict with the American Humanist Association. Naturalistic Humanism is our position."
>
> Barnes and Rosenfeld question whether a secular religion is possible. Not to make any one word too important, one could argue that today's Unitarian Universalism is a secular religion....
>
> Now for expediency. In the Torcaso case the court recognized Buddhism, Taoism, Ethical Culture and Secular Humanism as religions existing in the United States which do not teach what is traditionally considered belief in God. We should at least ask ourselves whether there are not practical advantages to be had by accepting this decision.

And so, to Wilson, and many other humanists, "secular religion" was not a contradiction in terms. The words defined a nontheistic faith. Comments by readers of the articles appeared in the January-February 1963 issue. Opinion was divided. The hard-core atheists objected to the use of the word "religion," while the Unitarians agreed with Wilson.

Humanist Manifesto II

In 1973 the humanists produced *Humanist Manifesto II*, an affirmation of the earlier document with updated views on the world's social problems. The new Manifesto was as hostile to traditional theistic religion as the earlier one. It said:

> As in 1933, humanists still believe that traditional theism, especially faith in the prayer-hearing God, assumed to love and care for persons, to hear and understand their prayers, and to be able to do something about them, is an unproved and outmoded faith. Salvationism, based on mere affirmation, still appears as harmful, diverting people with false hopes of heaven hereafter. Reasonable minds look to other means for survival....
>
> We believe...that traditional dogmatic or authoritarian religions that place revelation, God, ritual, or creed above human needs and experience do a disservice to the human species.... We find insufficient evidence for belief in the existence of a supernatural; it is either meaningless or irrelevant to the question of the survival and fulfillment of the human race. As nontheists, we begin with humans not God, nature not deity....
>
> [W]e can discover no divine purpose or providence for the human species. While there is much that we do not know, humans are responsible for what we are or will become. No deity will save us; we must save ourselves.

Ethics and Sex

Manifesto II also spelled out the social and political agendas for humanists:

> We affirm that moral values derive their source from human experience. Ethics is *autonomous* and *situational*, needing no theological or ideological sanction.... We strive for the good life, here and now....

> In the area of sexuality, we believe that intolerant attitudes, often cultivated by orthodox religions and puritanical cultures, unduly repress sexual conduct. The right to birth control, abortion, and divorce should be recognized.... Short of harming others or compelling them to do likewise, individuals should be permitted to express their sexual proclivities and pursue their life-styles as they desire.

Humanists also believe that civil liberties must include "a recognition of an individual's right to die with dignity, euthanasia, and the right to suicide."

World Government

The humanists again committed themselves to the goal of World Government. Manifesto II states:

> We deplore the division of humankind on nationalistic grounds. We have reached a turning point in human history where the best option is to *transcend the limits of national sovereignty* and to move toward the building of a world community in which all sectors of the human family can participate. Thus we look to the development of a system of world law and a world order based upon transnational federal government.

Anyone who bothers to study the curriculum of American public education will find in virtually every course and program the tremendous influence of humanist philosophy. It almost seems as if the public schools have become the parochial schools of humanism wherein American youngsters are aggressively indoctrinated in humanist values and ideas.

In fact, humanist editor Joe R. Burnett suggested as much in the November-December 1961 issue of *The Humanist* (p. 347) when arguing in favor of federal aid to education. He said:

> Humanists obviously have a vital interest in the passage of a strong bill for federal aid to public education. Without wanting to push the analogy too far, one might say that public education is the parochial education for scientific humanism.

If that was the case in 1961, it is even more so today.

Conclusion

Public education today is a government-supported establishment of the humanist religion.

Sources

Manifesto excerpts are from *Humanist Manifestos I and II*, published by Prometheus Books, 923 Kensington Avenue, Buffalo, New York 14215.

Homeschooling: The Real Revolution

Liberal political analyst Michael Lind writes in the opening chapter of his book, *Up from Conservatism*:

> American conservatism is dead. This is not to say that the conservative movement in American political history is over. Just as left-liberal Democrats continued to advance their agenda in the 1970s and 1980s — years after their ideology degenerated into an empty creed — so the right wing of the Republican Party may continue to expand its influence for some time to come. But those victories will be a result of external factors — the collapse of the left, the disorientation of the political center, the long-term conversion of the white South to the GOP, inertia — not of vigor or dynamism on the part of conservatives.... The project of sustaining a mainstream, centrist conservatism distinct from the far right in its positions, and not merely in its style, has failed.

Lind is perfectly right in describing "centrist conservatism" as lacking vigor or dynamism. Moderate Republicans are in essence liberals. Centrist conservatives are not revolutionaries or radicals. It is hard to describe what they actually are, except as careful politicians with a tepid free-enterprise agenda, political pragmatists. You have to go outside Congress and the political system to find the true freedom movement in America: the homeschool phenomenon. There is no other movement in America that has done more to recapture the spirit of American freedom than homeschooling.

Homeschoolers are, without question, revolutionary; they are making a clean break with the statist institution of government education. It is government-owned and -controlled education which is the very foundation of the secular state which exerts its power by molding the minds of its youngest citizens to serve the mythical state.

The Founders and the "State"

The Founding Fathers never created a "state" which had certain mystical powers over its citizens. That kind of state was a concept concocted in the mind of the German philosopher Hegel, a pantheist, who saw the State as God on earth. The Germans have always had a rather mystical view of the state and its power over the lives of its people, or "volk."

In America, this Hegelian state has evolved into something that simply cannot be made compatible with the American idea of government. Thus, when American courts speak of a compelling state interest in education without defining the state, or what is meant by *compelling*, or *education*, the assumption is that Americans regard the state as some sort of higher godlike power that must be served. The state they are talking about is the mystical Hegelian state.

What we have in America is a government, not a "state" in the Hegelian sense. We have a government run by men who must conform to a Constitution which places limits on what the government can do. There are no limits to what the Hegelian state can do, a fact tragically demonstrated during the Nazi era. In addition, we have a constitutional republic, not a democracy. A democracy is simply majority rule. A republic, through its written constitution, limits what the majority can do to the minority. Representatives, elected by the citizenry, are obliged to adhere to the limits placed on them by the Constitution.

Most Americans speak of our government as a democracy. They have virtually no understanding of the profound difference between a democracy and a constitutional republic. This gross lack of understanding is the work of the statist education system which has a vested interest in keeping Americans ignorant of the true role of limited government. The mystical "will of the people" is now what is considered to be the essence of American democracy. The "will of the people" has now become the sacred mantra of the humanist state as long as the will of the people can be manipulated by the humanist dominated media.

Christian Homeschooling

The homeschool revolution was started by Christians who recognized the implicit conflict that exists between Biblical religion and secular humanism. When it became obvious to them that the government schools had been thoroughly captured by the humanists, these parents had no choice but to remove their children from them. And inasmuch as many private schools have been greatly influenced by humanist philosophy, these Christian parents found it necessary to do the educating themselves. Also, many of them were strongly motivated to follow God's commandments concerning the education of children as given in Deuteronomy 6.

While religion was the primary moving force behind the early homeschoolers, they were also well aware of the academic decline within the public schools which no longer knew how to teach such basic subjects as reading or arithmetic. After all, it was in April 1983 that the National Commission on Excellence in Education issued its now historic report, stating: "If an unfriendly foreign power had attempted to impose on America the mediocre educational performance that exists today, we might well have viewed it as an act of war. As it stands, we have allowed this to happen to ourselves." Sixteen years later, the schools are probably worse today than they were then.

Homeschooling Pioneers

These early homeschoolers were the pioneers in the movement. They were generally well-educated orthodox Christians who understood the political and cultural forces at work, and were willing to take the necessary steps to guard their children against the growing moral and academic chaos in the public schools. In the 1960s and 70s, they were a tiny minority, and they tended to keep low profiles. However, whenever they were dragged into court by local superintendents who asserted implicitly that the children were owned by the state, ministers like Rev. Rousas J. Rushdoony were called by the homeschoolers to defend their God-given right to educate their children at home.

Those were the days before the creation of the Home School Legal Defense Association (HSLDA). The pioneers, like the Founding Fathers, tended to be strong people, willing to accept the consequences of their actions, but also willing to fight for their right to control and minister their own children's education. And the law and tradition were basically on their side. There were no federal laws preventing homeschooling and, in fact, education was not even mentioned in the U. S. Constitution. Also, most state compulsory school attendance laws provided room for exemptions.

Nevertheless, here and there, local judges, backed up by the education establishment, ordered local police to actually drag children away from their families in conformity with the state's supposed compelling interest in education. That's what happened in Plymouth County, Idaho, in 1985. In such cases, the public and even the liberal media tended to sympathize with the homeschoolers. News pictures of perfectly decent children being dragged away from their parents were not good PR for the school authorities.

Some parents actually went to jail. That was the case with the Pangelians who in 1985 spent 132 days in jail in Morgan County, Alabama, because they had decided to homeschool their children without the school district's approval and refused to turn their children over to the state authorities when ordered. Again, jailing Christian parents for homeschooling did not make good PR for state officials.

Two years later, after the ordeal was over, Sharon Pangelian was asked why she and her husband didn't take the children and leave Alabama. She wrote:

> That question was asked of us over and over before the trial. (And would continue to be asked during our time in jail, and even after we were released.) We answered the question the same way, over and over again: We don't want to be separated from our children at all. But if we run away, we teach them that courage has no part in liberty. If what you're doing is right, according to Scripture, then you don't run away. Fighting against oppression and ungodly usurpation of authority is indeed Scriptural, especially when it concerns the family.

That is the kind of courage and spiritual strength that undergirded the pioneers of the homeschool movement. In 1983, three homeschooling lawyers formed the Home School Legal Defense Association, "born out of the need to defend the growing number of homeschool families in each of our respective communities," writes Michael Farris, president of the HSLDA, who is also an ordained Baptist minister.

By 1990, more than 15,000 homeschoolers in all fifty states had joined the HSLDA, which offered legal services to homeschooling families who were experiencing legal difficulties in their communities.

A Thriving Movement

Today, the homeschool movement is thriving in a manner which would have been inconceivable twenty years ago. State homeschool organizations now have to rent large convention centers in which to hold their annual conventions which draw thousands of interested parents. Apparently, there is more to homeschooling than merely removing one's children from the morally corrupt public schools. There is now the sense that the new family lifestyle, which develops around homeschooling, is highly desirable because of the positive bonding it creates between parents and children. This is a particular blessing for the Christian family that seeks to live in conformity with Biblical truth, which is more easily imparted to their children.

While the early homeschoolers were considered pioneers, the families that followed were looked upon as settlers. The settlers created the state organizations, support groups, magazines, books, and curricula that have evolved into what one can call the homeschool academic and political establishment. While they have a long way to go before they can equal the National Education Association in political power, the exponential growth of the homeschool movement assures that its influence will be felt in the state legislatures and the Congress of tomorrow.

Today's newcomers to homeschooling are more like refugees, fleeing the failed government schools. They eagerly seek help from the settlers who are more than happy to provide it. But we should not be overly sanguine about the movement's success. The vast majority of Christians still put their children in the public schools. Also, many parents are seeking salvation in the new charter schools and the possible enactment of government voucher programs. They have yet to be weaned from the government trough. Nevertheless, the homeschool movement as it exists today represents a triumph of parental independence and enterprise. Christians must do all in their power to support it.

Let's Break Up the Public School Monopoly!

There, we've said it! We've mentioned the unmentionable. We've thought the unthinkable. Let's get the government out of the education business! It never belonged there in the first place. Let's privatize American education, from primary school to graduate school.

Much has been written about the privatization revolution. But the one area of our economy where privatization is needed more than in any other — education — has virtually been neglected by the privatizers. Why? Probably because public education is so entrenched in our society, such a sacred cow, supported by such politically powerful special interests that the idea of privatizing public education is considered impossible, impractical, beyond the pale, or an idea before its time.

Yet, the Secretary of Education, Lauro Cavazos, has warned us that unless our education system does better, "we may perish as the nation we know." Unless we believe the Secretary is blowing smoke, we'd better take his warning seriously.

But there is no indication whatever that the public schools will do better. In fact, the indications are that they will do worse, much worse. How do we know? We read what the educators write. We read those insufferably boring journals of education that pour out of the graduate schools like green slime, written in convoluted, professional jargon that cannot be understood by ordinary mortals. We read them, not because we want to, but because that's the only way to find out what the "educators" are really up to. And so we have no illusions about their ability or even willingness to "reform" education in a manner that will truly improve student performance.

The Only Solution

And so, after twenty years of studying this mess called public education, we've come to the conclusion that the only solution to America's perpetual education crisis is privatization. In other words, it is the government's intrusion into education which has politicized it to the point where it is impervious to true reform. The simple truth is that a government education system serves the government, not the children or their parents.

The idea that a government school system would serve the government is not a new idea. It was in the minds of those who envisioned public education before it was even in existence. As far back as 1826, James G. Carter, one of the leading proponents of state owned and operated schools, foresaw the importance of state controlled teachers colleges. He wrote:

> An institution for this purpose would become, by its influence on society, and particularly on the young,

> an engine to sway the public sentiment, the public morals, and the public religion, more powerful than any other in the possession of government.... It should emphatically be the State's institution.[1]

An Instrument of Government

And even earlier, in 1813, Robert Owen, the father of Socialism, wrote:

> It follows that every state, to be well governed, ought to direct its chief attention to the formation of character, and that the best governed state will be that which shall possess the best national system of education.
>
> Under the guidance of minds competent to its direction, a national system of training and education may be formed, to become the most safe, easy, effectual, and economical instrument of government that can be devised.[2]

It is significant that our Founding Fathers, with only a few exceptions, did not share such views. They regarded education to be a parental responsibility, best left in the hands of those morally and academically qualified to provide it. For that reason, early American education was largely private, efficient, practical, and realistic. Neither time nor money was wasted, and the result was that Americans had the highest literacy of any people on earth.

Today, our decline in literacy is a national scandal.

A Failed Monopoly

There is no cogent reason why the government should own or operate schools, colleges, and universities. The government monopoly is costly, wasteful, inefficient, and academically deficient. As David Kearns, chairman of the Xerox corporation, has said of public education, it is "a failed monopoly," producing workers "with a fifty percent defect rate." He complained that businesses must hire workers who can't read, write or count and then spend $25 billion a year to train them.[3]

The irony is that there are plenty of good private schools, colleges and universities in America, providing excellent education at no cost to the taxpayer and, for the most part, at moderate cost to the users.

Some people will claim that tax exemption costs the taxpayer indirectly; and it is true that government funds through student loans and research grants do help some private institutions. But the amount is infinitesimal compared to what the government schools cost the taxpayer. Moreover, private schools could do without that money if they had to.

Perhaps if the government schools were doing a decent job of teaching, taxpayers would feel that their money was being put to good use. But the public school system in America is a disaster. In fact, it is the only American institution that threatens our very future as a nation.

In addition, it is a monopoly, and monopolies are supposed to be bad. The court broke up AT&T because it was a monopoly and thwarted competition. AT&T was providing excellent service at moderate rates, and yet the court ruled that it had to be broken up because it was a monopoly.

Monopolies Distort Economies

Why are monopolies bad? They are bad because (1) they rely on government force for their existence; (2) they can set prices arbitrarily, and the consumer has no choice but to pay; (3) they do not reflect market values; (4) they distort the marketplace for the services or products they offer; (5) they create vested interests in the status quo; (6) they protect the inefficient; (7) they stand in the way of any improvement or invention that would make them obsolete; (8) they attract lovers of power rather than lovers of efficiency; (9) they create artificial values the consumer is forced to pay for; (10) they resent and try to eliminate competition; (11) they become self-serving; (12) and as their productivity and usefulness decline, they are driven to gain control of the very government that created them in order to insure their continued existence and prosperity. In short, their tendency is to become the public's master rather than the public's servant.

What makes government monopoly education even more dangerous to American freedom is the fact that it is largely controlled by a second private monopoly — the National Education Association — the nation's largest union, with a membership of close to two million.

Anyone who doubts the monopolistic character of the NEA ought to read their resolutions passed at their national conventions. Their goal is total power over the teaching profession — public and private. They are particularly hostile to private education, especially home education which they regard as a potential threat to their scheme for monopoly power. They have politicized the teachers of America in order to control the government that makes their monopoly possible. They represent the greatest organized threat to educational freedom and parents' rights in America today.

Unions Support Monopoly Education

It is true that the American Federation of Teachers represents a rival union. But it simply is no match for the NEA. In any case, both unions provide powerful support for government monopoly education. Without that monopoly, the unions themselves would lose much of their political influence.

Thus, American education and American children have become the victims of two monopolies that clearly violate the principles of the antitrust laws. These laws reflect the public's abhorrence of monopoly. Why aren't they being enforced? Why are these monopolies tolerated when their very existence makes educational reform impossible? Why? Because of ignorance and indifference.

But we ought not to be indifferent to a system that is costing the taxpayers $200 billion a year and turning out functional illiterates by the million. The very existence of a growing underclass of people in our inner cities, condemned to lives of poverty and hopelessness, is proof that government monopoly education is a colossal failure, unable to perform its minimal task of educating the poor.

Thus far, all attempts to reform the system have resulted in even greater failure. The fifty billion dollars the federal government has poured into compensatory education (Title One) since 1965 has resulted in lower SAT scores and more illiteracy, not less.

Consumers Lose

Government monopoly education is no more capable of delivering the goods in America than are the failed economic monopolies in the communist countries. Economies that are not accountable to the consumer have no incentives to produce values, for they themselves are consumers of the taxpayers' wealth rather than producers of new wealth in their own right.

Why can't the system deliver excellence? Are there not decent, dedicated teachers in the public schools? Yes, there are. But they will be the first to point out how difficult it is to produce excellence in the system. Marva Collins is a case in point.

Mrs. Collins taught in the public schools of Chicago for fourteen years and found the task so frustrating that she quit the public system and created a private school of her own which has achieved national recognition and fame for the academic excellence it produces.

Is there not a lesson to be learned from Mrs. Collins' experience?

Benefits of Privatization

Privatizing American education would result in enormous benefits:

1. Taxpayers would be relieved of a huge tax burden, permitting them to use their money in more productive ways.

2. The cost of education would decline dramatically. In 1989, the average cost per pupil in the public schools was about $4,500. In 2002, that cost is from $6,000 to $10,000. There are many private schools that charge half as much and provide better education.

3. Education would improve. There is no doubt that when educators are accountable to the consumer who pays the bills, the education they deliver must be of a quality acceptable to the customer. Free competition among private schools would force schools to strive for better quality education. Also, education would be redefined in more realistic, practical terms than in the utopian, vaguely messianic terms of statist philosophers.

4. Privatization would eliminate the cultural and religious conflicts that now plague public education. Parents should be free to obtain the kind of education they want for their children: religious, secular, special, denominational, etc. Each school would offer its philosophy of education, and parents would know what they were getting.

5. Privatization would promote educational freedom, which in turn would promote greater appreciation of political and economic freedom, greater diversity, greater opportunity. Privatization would strengthen the principles of freedom that form the basis of America's social and political culture.

6. Privatization would open an entire new field for free enterprise and technology. Chain schools, franchises, homeschool networks would produce a

whole new, exciting world of activity, new opportunities for economic growth. Just as the breakup of AT&T has led to an explosion of new inventions and opportunities in telecommunications, a breakup of government monopoly education would unleash the creative drive of thousands of entrepreneurs. We actually know more about how children learn than ever before, but the government schools cannot make use of this knowledge or the new technology that would enhance education.

7. Privatization would solve many of our social problems caused by poor government education. Illiteracy produces delinquency, crime, poverty. Private schools would provide individuals with the academic skills needed to function in our hi-tech economy. Social welfare costs would begin to decline instead of continuing to rise. We would stop the growth of that urban cancer known as the underclass.

8. Privatization would also improve the lives of children. Better educated, motivated children are less likely to get into trouble than those victimized by educational malpractice, drugs, gangs, etc. Private schools are in a better position to protect children than the public schools.

9. Literacy would improve, for private schools would use reading instruction programs that work. Today, reading instruction in public schools is provided by professionals who are more interested in "theories" about how children learn to read than in how they actually learn to read. Privatization would solve our literacy problem in a very short time.

10. Privatization would permit schools to teach religion and thereby improve the moral behavior of American children.

11. Privatization would represent a sharp rebuke to the philosophy of statism, the idea that the state owns the children and therefore can compel them to attend government schools for indoctrination. A government school system implies the existence of a government sanctioned philosophy of education. It is not the business of government to devise a philosophy of education which all must accept. But since it is impossible to conduct education without a philosophy behind it, the government has no choice but to become a philosopher — which it is not fitted to be.

12. Privatization would depoliticize education and make it a consumer value subject to market forces rather than political influences. It would return educators to the business of education.

13. Privatization would end the battles and schemes of different groups contending to control the system for the purpose of advancing their own social and political agendas.

14. Privatization would reduce the size and cost of government by eliminating all of the bureaucracies that presently run the government schools.

15. Privatization would liberate American education from the clutches of self-styled experts and professionals who have turned the present system into the academic swamp it has become.

16. Privatization would force a thorough shake up of all that we call education and eventually result in an education system brought down to earth, manageable in its private increments, subject to all the improvements that human ingenuity in freedom can devise.

17. Privatization of teacher training would liberate the profession from the heavy hand of bureaucratic control and artificial requirements. Private education would make teaching once more a joy instead of a nightmare.

It is obvious that only through privatization could American education once more become rational, workable, accountable, cost efficient, academically sound, and user friendly. Instead of being the intellectual crippler it is today, American education would become a dynamic, exciting, diverse, open, responsive institution, accommodating the needs of children in a free society.

What About the Poor?

The question is always asked: how would the poor be educated in a totally private system? The answer is quite simple. There would be more than enough resources available from foundations, philanthropies and communities to pay the tuition of poor children. Let us make it possible for poor children to get as good an education in a private school as their parents want.

How can privatization take place? First, there would have to be a consensus among business leaders and enlightened citizens that privatization is the only solution that will work, the only way to end our endless educational crisis. When that happens, the unthinkable will then become thinkable, and ways will be devised to privatize the system. State constitutions may have to be amended. Bureaucracies will have to be closed down, school buildings sold, new private schools built, etc. Union resistance will have to be overcome. A very tall order.

Can it be done? Only if the American people will it.

And if they don't will it, they will continue to suffer the agonies, the costs, the indignities of a system that doesn't work and, as the Secretary has warned, could cause the destruction of America as we have known it.

Footnotes

[1] Carter, James G., "Outline of an Institution for the Education of Teachers," *Essays on Popular Education* (Boston, 1826.) pp. 47-51

[2] Owen, Robert, *A New View of Society or Essays on the Formation of the Human Character* (London, 1816.)

[3] *USA Today*, October 27, 1987.

Deliberately Dumbing Us Down

Charlotte Thomson Iserbyt's new book, *The Deliberate Dumbing Down of America*, is without doubt one of the most important publishing events in the annals of American education in the last hundred years. John Dewey's *School and Society*, published in 1899, set American education on its course to socialism. Rudolf Flesch's *Why Johnny Can't Read*, published in 1955, informed American parents that there was something terribly wrong with the way the schools were teaching children to read, and my own book, *NEA: Trojan Horse in American Education*, published in 1984, explained in great detail how and why the decline in public education was taking place.

But Iserbyt has done what no one else wanted or could do. She has put together the most formidable and practical compilation of documentation describing the well-planned "deliberate dumbing down" of American children by their education system. Anyone who has had any lingering hope that what the educators have been doing is a result of error, accident, or stupidity will be shocked by the way American social engineers have systematically gone about destroying the intellect of millions of American children for the purpose of leading the American people into a socialist world government controlled by behavioral and social scientists.

This mammoth book is the size of a large city phone book: 462 pages of documentation, 205 pages of appendices, and a 48-page index. The documentation is "A Chronological Paper Trail" which starts with the "Sowing of the Seeds" in the late eighteenth and nineteenth centuries, proceeds to "The Turning of the Tides," then to "The Troubling Thirties," "The Fomentation of the Forties and Fifties," "The Sick Sixties," "The Serious Seventies," "The 'Effective' Eighties," and finally, "The Noxious Nineties." The educators and social engineers indict themselves with their own words.

Iserbyt decided to compile this book because, as a "resister" to what is going on in American education, she was being constantly told that she was taking things out of context. The book, she writes, "was put together primarily to satisfy my own need to see the various components which led to the dumbing down of the United States of America assembled in chronological order — in writing. Even I, who had observed these weird activities taking place at all levels of government, was reluctant to accept a malicious intent behind each individual, chronological activity or innovation, unless I could connect it with other, similar activities taking place at other times."

And that is what this book does. It connects educators, social engineers, planners, government grants, federal and state agencies, billion-dollar foundations, think tanks, universities, research projects, policy organizations, etc., showing how they have worked together to advance an agenda that will change America from a free republic to a socialist state.

What is so mind boggling is that all of this is being financed by the American people themselves through their own taxes. In other words, the American people are underwriting the destruction of their own freedom and way of life by lavishly financing through federal and state grants the very social scientists who are undermining our national sovereignty and preparing our children to become the dumbed-down vassals of the new world order.

One of the interesting insights revealed by these documents is how the social engineers use a deliberately created education "crisis" to move their agenda forward by offering radical reforms that are sold to the public as fixing the crisis — which they never do. The new reforms simply set the stage for the next crisis, which provides the pretext for the next move forward. This is the dialectical process at work, a process our behavioral engineers have learned to use very effectively. Its success depends on the ability of the "change agents" to continually deceive the public, which tends to believe any lie the experts tell them.

Iserbyt's long journey to becoming a "resister" started in 1973 when her son, a fourth grader, brought home from school a purple ditto sheet, embellished with a smiley face, entitled, "All About Me." She writes, "The questions were highly personal; so much so that they encouraged my son to lie, since he didn't want to 'spill the beans' about his mother, father and brother. The purpose of such a questionnaire was to find out the student's state of mind, how he felt, what he liked and disliked, and what his values were. With this knowledge it would be easier for the government school to modify his values and behavior at will — without, of course, the student's knowledge or his parents' consent."

From that time on, Iserbyt became an activist in education. She became a member of a philosophy committee for a school, was elected as a school board member, co-founded Guardians of Education for Maine (GEM), and finally became senior policy advisor in the Office of Educational Research and Improvement (OERI) of the U.S. Department of Education during President Reagan's first term of office.

As a school board member she learned that in American education, the end justifies the means. "Our change agent superintendent," she writes, "was more at home with a lie than he was with the truth." Whatever good she accomplished while on the school board was tossed out two weeks after she left office.

It was during her tenure in the Department of Education in Washington, D.C., where she had access to the grant proposals from change agents, that she came to the conclusion that what was happening in American education was the result of a concerted effort on the part of numerous individuals and organizations — a globalist elite — to bring about permanent changes in America's body politic. She was relieved of her duties after leaking an important technology grant — a computer-assisted instruction proposal — to the press.

Another reason why Iserbyt decided to publish this book is because of the reluctance of Americans to face unpleasant truths about their government educators. She wants parents to have access to the kinds of documents that were only circulated among the change agent educators themselves. She wants parents to see for themselves what has been planned for their children and the kind of socialist-fascist world their children will have to live in if we do nothing to counter these plans.

Therefore, getting this book into the hands of thousands of Americans ought to be a major project for lovers of liberty in the year 2000. It will do more to defeat the change agents than anything else I can think of.

From New Deal to Raw Deal

Recently I came across an interesting book, *A New Deal*, by Stuart Chase, published in 1932. This is the book that not only gave Franklin Delano Roosevelt a blueprint for leading America toward socialism, but it also gave that program a name: the New Deal. The book was a no-holds-barred attack on capitalism and an argument for a controlled economy. Chase wrote:

> Feudalism, for all its harsh fixity, had a sense of function. Both noble and priest recognized, if they did not always practice, social responsibility. The curse of laissez-faire and its cousin capitalism is that responsibility is removed. Having made his money, the entrepreneur's work is done. ... Laissez-faire is barren of a sense of state, and its chief ornaments are, beyond their safes and counters, lost and homeless men.... [Laissez-faire] exalted the worst side of human nature — greed and acquisitiveness.

What an incredibly distorted view of laissez-faire, the great and exhilarating idea of economic freedom — the wish to be left alone by government. According to Chase, the problem with economic freedom is that it is unpredictable. It can produce radical change and economic instability overnight through new inventions. For example, the invention of the automobile changed America from top to bottom in just a few short years. Such unfettered change exasperated Chase. He wrote:

> It would be a jolly good thing to declare a moratorium on inventions for at least a decade, and treat all inventors as dangerous lunatics, with proper care and supervision. ... One of the best hopes for securing real progress in the future is to bottle up technical progress, and feed it out with a measuring cup.

Although Chase abhorred the radical changes that technology created in a capitalist system, he had no objection to radical economic and political upheaval through bloody revolution, concerning which he wrote:

> I believe it to have been necessary and inevitable in Russia. It may some day be inevitable in this country. I am not seriously alarmed by the sufferings of the creditor class, the troubles which the church is bound to encounter, the restrictions on certain kinds of freedom which must result, nor even by the bloodshed of the transition period. A better economic order is worth a little bloodshed.

Of course, in 1932, one could still be giddy about the thought of revolution as a welcome relief from liberal boredom. It is estimated that Russia's "better economic order" cost about sixty million lives. A little bloodshed indeed! And then there was Pol Pot also seeking a "better economic order." Of course, we now have sixty-plus years of hindsight with which to evaluate Chase's glib ideas which had such enormous influence among the New Dealers. But Chase also realized that there was a spiritual dimension that had to be addressed. He wrote:

> Finally, revolution can give what no other road promises to give so directly and forcibly — a new religion. It will be based not on rewards in the Hereafter, but on peace, goodwill and plenty on earth today.... Great religious movements have usually been grounded in collectivism, in the brotherhood of man, leaving laissez-faire, in the last analysis, a cold and ferocious anti-Christ.... Western mankind is thirsty for something in which to believe again. Red revolution is a creed, dramatic, idealistic and, in the long run, constructive.

What was Chase's solution for America? A controlled economy. He explains it in a chapter entitled, "Control from the Top":

> The drive of collectivism leads toward control from the top. A managed currency demands a board of managers; long-term government budgeting demands expert technical supervision with special reference to the income tax; a minimum wage law demands economists and statisticians to set the minimums; the control of foreign investments demands a competent authority on which investors and the public can rely. The regulation of hours of labor, of minors in industry, the creation of a scheme for unemployment insurance, an augmented public works program, the control of domestic investment, indeed nearly every plank in our platform leads directly to a conning tower or

> series of conning towers which must see the nation steadily and see it whole.

The New Deal gave us all of that, and LBJ's Great Society expanded federal control even further. Hillary Clinton and her gang wanted even more federal expansion into a complete takeover of the healthcare system. They were stopped by their own arrogance and incompetence. The American people would have probably accepted socialized medicine had it not been shoved in their faces by the radical leftists on Hillary's team. The nation is now discussing federal payments for drug prescriptions. If that isn't socialism, what is?

Chase knew that his plans would encounter resistance. He wrote:

> Woe to Supreme Courts, antiquated rights of property, checks and balances and democratic dogmas which stand in the path. We shall have plenty of exhilaration on the road if we have the will and courage to take it, even if it lacks the drama of red dictatorships and the imperial eagles of the black.

Chase was counting on "a million intelligent Americans" to bring about the change by organizing in every community in the nation. He writes, "The funny thing about it is that the groups are actually beginning to form.... They are part of what H. G. Wells has called the Open Conspiracy. Why should Russians have all the fun of remaking a world?"

The gulag, of course, was great fun! That's the kind of intellectual lunacy that has brought America to its present state of federal control over our lives. The liberals will not let up on their drive toward a totally controlled society, despite the record of death and destruction their socialist ideas have visited on millions of human beings across the planet.

Resistance to all of this is growing by the day as more and more Americans see socialist incrementalism threatening more and more of their freedoms. In 1964, 26 million Americans voted for Goldwater despite the heaviest media barrage in U.S. elective history. Today, with the Internet providing freedom lovers with the means to reach millions of their fellow citizens, there is more than just hope that the drive toward total government can be stopped. All it really requires is strict adherence to the Constitution of the United States. But it will take an intelligent and alert minority of Americans to organize, educate, and run for office to make things really happen.

The Century That Was

In a few short weeks, the twentieth century will be history, and editors of establishment magazines and newspapers will be asking noted historians, usually from the Council on Foreign Relations or its academic equivalents, to evaluate the century that was. One such evaluation has already been given by liberal historian Arthur Schlesinger Jr. in the December 1999 issue of the *AARP Bulletin*. The AARP, as everyone knows, is the American Association of Retired Persons. But that's a misnomer, since many members of the AARP are not retired but continue to work at their various professions. The organization ought to change its name to the American Association of Recipients of Social Security Payments, because that's what most of its members over sixty-five all have in common.

Getting back to the century that will soon — and none too soon — be gone, Schlesinger entitled his article, "The Glorious and the Damned." The rubric under which the article was published is "Witness to the Century." Since all of the members of the AARP have been witnesses to the century, we all have our own views of it. But since the AARP is run by liberals, the slant given in that journal is a liberal one and reflects the views of liberal Democrats rather than conservative Republicans. In fact, one of the most ferocious political struggles of this century in the U.S. has been that between liberals and conservatives, and it will no doubt continue into the twenty-first century with a vengeance.

As early as 1932, Walter Lippmann was writing about the political struggle between the "internationalists" and the "isolationists." The latter were the Republican presidents who followed internationalist Woodrow Wilson after the end of World War I. The American people had wanted to get back to the way things were before the war. But the internationalists were determined to keep America involved with Europe. Through their control of the Federal Reserve System, they were able to create and then use the Great Depression to get rid of the Republican so-called isolationists. Franklin D. Roosevelt brought the internationalists back into the White House, and they've been there ever since.

Liberals have a view of the century defined by the very vocabulary they use, and we find that that vocabulary gives us an insight into the philosophical mindset of Mr. Schlesinger. His hero, of course, is Franklin D. Roosevelt, who gave us the New Deal, the beginnings of a socialist society, and provided the leadership that led us to victory in World War II. Schlesinger writes:

> No leader brought out the best of the 20th century more effectively than Franklin D. Roosevelt. In striving for his objectives, FDR could be tricky,

> manipulative and tough. But these objectives amounted to the emancipation of humanity. He defined them best in 1941 when he set forth the Four Freedoms — Freedom of Speech and Expression, Freedom of Worship, Freedom from Want, Freedom from Fear. These remain humanity's vital purposes today.

Thus, from a liberal point of view, the United States government must concern itself not merely with the well-being of the American people but of "humanity." The Four Freedoms, as presented by FDR, imply that freedoms are granted by governments, when in reality, the American constitutional system is based on the understanding that all men are endowed by their Creator with certain inalienable rights, and that the purpose of government is to secure these rights: life, liberty, and the pursuit of happiness. Freedom of speech and religion were written into our Bill of Rights, because it was understood that governments have a tendency to deprive people of their basic rights.

How can any government guarantee freedom from fear? Most governments create fear. Before the income tax, Americans were not afraid of their government. Now they are. The threat of an audit creates fear.

How can any government guarantee freedom from want? According to our system, it is the unalienable right and responsibility of every adult to provide food, clothing, and shelter for himself and his loved ones. Apart from natural disasters, governments are the powers that usually create starvation and destruction. Schlesinger acknowledges that it is the creative energy of a free people that has given us the economic wealth that we enjoy. But he attributes it all to democracy. He writes:

> Where totalitarianism suppressed the individual, democracy empowers individuals, giving them the opportunity and the right to think and debate and invent and dream.

Again, the notion that governments grant rights to individuals. But our government — which is a republic and not a democracy — does not have the power to grant unalienable rights. That power belongs to God alone, who endowed us with unalienable rights. Our struggle has always been against governments that have time and again wanted to deprive citizens from exercising their unalienable rights. And we can see that happening today as government is doing all in its power to deprive Americans of their unalienable right to own the means of defending themselves with firearms. The Second Amendment was written into our Bill of Rights because of the understanding the Founding Fathers had of government power.

And whatever happened to the Right to Life? The right to kill the unborn has been granted by our democratic government to women who wish to dispose of unwanted babies in their wombs. But no one has an unalienable right to kill. A defenseless unborn child needs protection since our Declaration of Independence states quite plainly that the purpose of government is to secure the unalienable rights of its human citizens, which does not exclude the unborn, since all of us have been unborn at that stage of our development. Since being unborn is an unavoidable condition of being human, how can the state of being unborn make one eligible to be legally murdered?

The twentieth century was plagued by two horrible ideas: communism and utopianism, both very unbiblical. Communism, and its two other manifestations, socialism and Nazism, have been discredited. But utopianism is still very much with us in the idea of a socialist world government. It will be interesting to see how far into the twenty-first century that utopian dream — or nightmare — prevails.

The Meaning and Mystery of Numbers

On New Year's Eve, I, like so many other Americans, was glued to my TV set watching ABC and PBS take us to celebrations across the globe, beginning at some remote island in the South Pacific where the year 2000 started, then to New Zealand, Australia, Japan, China, Moscow, Bethlehem, Rome, Paris, London, Newfoundland, Rio de Janeiro, New York, Montreal, Toronto and Chicago. I did not stay up long enough to see the new year arrive in Los Angeles, or Honolulu, which was probably the last major city on earth to finally come into the year 2000.

It was amazing to see the delirium in Times Square as more than a million folk turned out to see the famous ball atop the Times building lowered so that the sign 2000 could light up. The only thing that changed after that momentous countdown was a number — from 1999 to 2000. Yet that immaterial, spiritual change of one number forced nations across the globe to spend billions of dollars on fireworks displays, parades, concerts, dances, celebrations, and feasts, all of which took years of preparation. My favorite displays were the fireworks on the Eiffel Tower in Paris. It lived up to all its hype. That tower, a culminating display of nineteenth century technology, has a grace, dignity, and solidity reflecting the inventive genius of that century.

Why is one number so important? Why is it capable of creating delirium among millions of celebrants? We are the only species who believe in the power of numbers. The Bible is full of numbers. There is even a Book of Numbers. There are Ten Commandments, Seven Seals, Twelve Tribes, Seven Angels. God gave man not only the ability to count, but the absolute necessity to count.

What are numbers? They are merely the names and written symbols we give to quantities. The need to count is what makes numbers necessary. We count everything. We count days, weeks, months, years, decades, centuries, millennia. We count the miles we travel and the number of hours and minutes it takes us to get from here to there. We count a hundredth of a second in Olympic races. We count our birthdays. The countdown of life begins at conception, nine months of gestation. Some lives are cut short before birth, before that developing human being has learned the meaning of numbers.

We register the day, month and year of birth and then count each completed year of life as a blessing. Last May, I completed seventy-three full years of life. My brain, like a computer, has a storehouse of memory which is now so full that sometimes it is slow in bringing up a name or a particular event. But memory is extremely useful in being able to recall what life was like fifty or sixty years ago. It gives one a view of a changing world that the young simply do not have. Reading about it is not like having been there. And most young people do not bother to read if, indeed, they can read.

And many young people have difficulty with numbers because of the way they are now taught in our public schools. Math test scores have been dismal. Why? Because the schools cannot deal with the mystery of numbers, which is really part of religion. For example, the delirium over the beginning of a new millennium is fraught with religious significance. The counting in our calendar is based on the birth of Jesus Christ, who was sent to this earth to save men from their sinful natures, to offer them forgiveness of sin, salvation and eternal life after death.

But humanists, who do not believe in Biblical religion, prefer to celebrate the New Year as the time in the calendar when the days begin getting longer. They simply see mankind as a species of animal living on a planet that revolves around the sun every 365 days or so, and rotates on an axis which gives us days and nights. They see no religious significance in any of this. They see no mystery in numbers.

But it is religion that has created meaning in numbers. The Lord created the universe in six days and rested on the seventh, which is why we have a week and a Sabbath weekend. We celebrate festivals that conform to Biblical commandments, requirements and events. God gave us a rudimentary calculator in our ten fingers. That is why we use a ten-base system of counting.

We also know that the marvelous technology that permitted us to place satellites in outer space so that we could view the New Year celebrations around the globe depended on the development of mathematics. All of computer technology is based on the ability of the human brain to translate numbers and letters into zeros and ones by way of electrical impulses. Even the concept of zero is one of the great inventions of the human brain, without which all of our modern technology would not have been possible.

Another important use of numbers is in the forming of chronological memory, on which all of our knowledge of history is based. In fact, the Bible itself is the standard of chronological narration, which begins with Day One of Creation and extends beyond the written word of Scripture to our present-day calendar of events. History can only be understood in chronological terms, for it permits us to analyze cause and effect. And that is why American children are deprived of a chronological study of American history — so that they will be unable to understand cause and effect. They are told that remembering dates is not important. It's no longer necessary to know what happened in 1492, 1776, 1789, 1860, 1917, 1939, 1941, or 1945.

I became acutely aware of the importance of chronology when I was researching my book, *Is Public Education Necessary?* I wanted to find out why the American people gave up educational freedom for government-owned and -operated schools so early in our nation's history when the advantages of educational freedom were so obvious in view of the fact that that is what our Founding Fathers enjoyed. I had to do a year-by-year investigation to finally understand how and why that change took place. It had nothing to do with economics or literacy. It was all philosophical, and that was a profound revelation to me. That philosophical revolution was engineered by a small Unitarian elite that had captured Harvard University and began its work of secularizing education through government ownership of schools. It was the beginning of political liberalism.

We need to know numbers in order to survive. We must count money. We must count taxes. We must count commodities. We must count billions and trillions in government spending. We must count people. In the Book of Numbers we find much counting of people of different ages for social, military and religious reasons. Civilized nations count themselves. Counting always answers the questions of how many, how long, how short, how high, how low.

And now we must start dating our checks, and letters, and diaries with the year 2000 or, if we prefer to use Roman numerals, MM. The human race has reached an incredible milestone when we think of what life was like in the year 1000. Most of the material advance that has so profoundly changed human life took place only in the last 150 years. The young have so much to look forward to, provided they don't forget that what they enjoy today is the result of what human beings did and invented before them. The past is, indeed, prelude.

Whole Language and the Future of Reading Instruction in America

In September 1993, the U.S. Education Department released the results of its fourteen million dollar survey of Adult Literacy in America. Some 26,000 adults were interviewed at length and their levels of literacy were calculated on a scale of 0 to 500. By extrapolating the results of those interviews, it is now estimated that some forty million American adults fall within the score range of 0 to 225, meaning that they have only the most rudimentary reading and writing skills. An additional fifty million adults fared a little better And only twenty percent — thirty-four to forty million adult Americans — can be considered to be fully literate.

The *New York Times* headline (9/9/93) read, "Study Says Half of Adults in U.S. Can't Read or Handle Arithmetic." The *Boston Globe* led the story with "Ninety million US adults called barely literate." You would think that such headlines would create a sense of crisis or urgency among our educators and political leaders. You would think that such news would call for a Congressional investigation. But the best we could get out of Education Secretary Richard Riley was, "This should be a wake-up call for all Americans to consider going back to school and getting a tune-up."

As if a "tune-up" is going to solve America's literacy crisis. Can you imagine Hillary Rodham Clinton calling for a "tune-up" to solve America's much publicized health crisis? And the government already owns and controls public education. In fact, we've had socialized education in America for over a hundred years!

None of the people who commented on the dire consequences of growing illiteracy in America — such as Labor Secretary Robert Reich or Keith Poston, spokesman for the National Alliance of Business, called for an investigation of teaching practices in our schools. None of them bothered to ask how is it possible to get such poor results when more children are spending more time in school than ever before at more cost to the taxpayer than ever before, and never have teachers been paid more, and never has the Federal government pumped more billions into educational research and compensatory education than ever before. So why the dismal results?

Well, we know why, and it was Rudolf Flesch who told us why back in 1955 with his famous book, *Why Johnny Can't Read.* Flesch told us that the reason why Johnny couldn't read was because of the faulty way in which he was being taught. He explained how in the early 1930s, the professors of education changed the way reading is taught in American schools. They threw out the traditional alphabetic-phonics method, which is the proper way to teach children to read an alphabetic writing system, and replaced it with a look-say whole-word, or sight method that teaches children to read English as if it were Chinese, an ideographic writing system. Flesch said that when you impose an ideographic teaching method on an alphabetic writing system, you get reading disability.

Even Dr. Seuss agreed with Flesch. In explaining to an interviewer for *Arizona* magazine in 1981 how he wrote the *Cat in the Hat,* he said:

> They think I did it in twenty minutes. That damned *Cat in the Hat* took nine months until I was satisfied. I did it for a textbook house and they sent me a word list. That was due to the Dewey revolt in the Twenties in which they threw out phonic reading and went to word recognition, as if you're reading Chinese pictographs instead of blending sounds of different letters. I think killing phonics was one of the greatest causes of illiteracy in the country.

And so, we've known now since 1955 that whole-word methodology is the problem. Flesch naively assumed back then that after the educators read his book they would recognize the error of their ways and return to the sane phonetic method of teaching. What he didn't understand, however, was the political agenda behind what those progressive professors were doing. Their goal was to use education as the means of changing America from an individualist, capitalist, religious society into a socialist, collectivist, humanist society. Ironically, Flesch himself was a socialist who believed that even little socialists should be able to read phonetically.

But it was John Dewey who identified high literacy as the main obstacle to socialism because it produced people with independent intelligence who could think for themselves, read the Bible, and act as individuals. Dewey said we needed a different kind of literacy, a socially based literacy that created interdependence in a collectivist society. The result was the introduction of the look-say, whole-word method which indeed produced a much lower level of functional literacy.

And so, in 1955, instead of admitting the error of their ways, the professors of reading did just the opposite. They founded the International Reading Association which became the fortress of the look-say method, protecting them and their publishers from the likes of Rudolf Flesch and other critics who would attack look-say in the future.

Now, whole language is a further development of the whole-word method. The main difference between the two is that whole-language educators have discarded the insipid Dick and Jane type basal readers in favor of "real literature," that is, trade books which usually include stories about ecology, environmentalism, witchcraft, the occult, and death. In other words, while both methods don't teach children to read phonetically, at least no child ever had nightmares after reading Dick and Jane, but many children are having nightmares from what they read in whole-language classes. But whole-language educators insist that whole language represents a new philosophy of reading.

It is also important to understand that whole language is an integral part of the education restructuring movement known as Outcome Based Education, and OBE reformers love to point out that OBE represents a paradigm shift in educational thinking. Bill Spady writes in his Outcome Based restructuring presentation:

> The advocates of this Transformational OBE paradigm are people whose thinking is future-oriented, visionary, optimistic, growth-oriented, and success-oriented. Educationally they embrace, rather than fear, change; and they are what futurist Joel Barker calls "paradigm pioneers."

And so, the promoters of OBE see themselves as "paradigm pioneers."

The 1986 edition of *Webster's New World Dictionary* (Simon & Schuster) defines paradigm as "a pattern, example, or model; an overall concept accepted by most people in an intellectual community, as a science, because of its effectiveness in explaining a complex process, idea, or set of ideas."

But it is obvious that our present-day educationists use the term to signify a fundamental change in values. Marilyn Ferguson, in her book, *The Aquarian Conspiracy* which is sort of a guide to New Age thinking and trends, uses the word *paradigm* throughout the book to signify a fundamental transformation that is taking place within our society on a technological as well as spiritual level, that is, a shift from a God-centered worldview to a pagan worldview. She doesn't quite put it as simply as I do. She writes under the heading "The Paradigm Shift":

> New perspectives give birth to new historic ages. Humankind has had many dramatic revolutions of understanding — great leaps, sudden liberation from old limits....
>
> New paradigms are nearly always received with coolness, even mockery and hostility.... The new perspective demands such a switch that established scientists are rarely converted.... When a critical number of thinkers has accepted the new idea, a collective paradigm shift has occurred.

So the notion of a paradigm shift is a powerful one when used to sell a new idea. That's the way it's being used to sell whole language and Outcome Based Education. But the word *paradigm* itself is a neutral term, and can be applied to Christian Reconstruction as well. To my mind the most significant paradigm shift taking place in education today is the idea that home education is not only superior to public education, but superior to K-12 formal schooling in general. That's a real paradigm shift being made by thousands of individual families all across America.

The point is that the advocates of whole language are using the idea of a paradigm shift to give the illusion that they are on the cutting edge of educational progress for the twenty-first century. But they are simply carrying out Dewey's plan to lower the literacy level of the American people.

That a dumbing down process has been going on in America has been recognized by many researchers. In fact, back in 1971, *Dallas Morning News* columnist David Hawkins did a column entitled "Young People Are Getting Dumber." In it he interviewed John Gaston, head of the Fort Worth branch of the Human Engineering Laboratory, which has specialized in aptitude testing since 1922. Gaston said:

> Do you know that the present generation knows less than its parents? All of our laboratories around the country are recording a drop in vocabulary of one percent a year. In all our fifty years of testing it's never happened before.... Young people know fewer words than their fathers. That makes them know less. Can you imagine what a drop in knowledge of one percent a year for thirty years could do to our civilization? We also believe that the recent rise in violence correlates with the drop in vocabulary. Long testing has convinced us that crime and violence predominate among people who score low in vocabulary. If they can't express themselves with their tongues, they'll use their fists.... We define intelligence as natural aptitudes plus knowledge, which is another word for vocabulary.... Brilliant aptitudes aren't worth much without words to give them wings. The one thing successful people have in common isn't high aptitudes — it's high vocabulary, and it's within everybody's reach.

Is look-say and whole language contributing to the dumbing down process? Let's take a look at whole language. Its advocates claim that its goal is not to produce an accurate reader. An article in the *Washington Post* of November 29, 1986 makes that very clear. The headline reads: "Reading Method Lets Pupils Guess; Whole-Language Approach Riles Advocates of Phonics." The article says:

> The most controversial aspect of whole language is the de-emphasis on accuracy. American Reading Council President Julia Palmer, an advocate of the approach, said it is acceptable if a young child reads the word *house* for *home*, or substitutes the word *pony* for *horse*. "It's not very serious because she understands the meaning," said Palmer. "Accuracy is not the name of the game."

We find the same idea stated in a book entitled *Evaluation: Whole Language, Whole Child* which was written by two whole language teachers. They write (pp. 18-19):

> Miscue analysis is a tool you can use to help you understand what strategies a child is employing while reading. It offers a new way of looking at language learning.... The way you interpret what the child does will reflect what you understand reading to be. For instance, if she reads the word *feather* for *father* a phonics-oriented teacher might be pleased because she's come close to sounding the word out. However, if you believe reading is a meaning-seeking process, you may be concerned that she's overly dependent on phonics at the expense of meaning. You'd be happier with a miscue such as *daddy* even though it doesn't look

> or sound anything like the word in the text. At least the meaning would be intact.

Well if we go along with what these teachers are saying, then a sentence like "Mother and I were having a discussion while waiting for father to get home from work" could be approvingly read as "Mummy and me were sitting around chewing the fat, waiting for popsy to come home from his job." The meaning would be intact. The only problem is that it is not what the author wrote. But apparently, that is no longer important to whole-language teachers. In fact, this is how whole-language advocates define reading. This is taken from a book entitled *Whole Language, What's the Difference* by three professors of education. They write (p. 19):

> From a whole language perspective, reading (and language use in general) is a process of generating hypotheses in a meaning-making transaction in a sociohistorical context. As a transactional process...reading is not a matter of "getting the meaning" from the text, as if that meaning were in the text waiting to be decoded by the reader. Rather, reading is a matter of readers using the cues print provides and the knowledge they bring with them (of language subsystems, of the world) to construct a unique interpretation. Moreover, that interpretation is situated: readers' creations (not retrievals) of meaning with text vary, depending on their purposes for reading and the expectations of others in the reading event. This view of reading implies that there is no single "correct" meaning for a given text, only plausible meanings.

Pretty ridiculous, isn't it? These poor souls don't even know the meaning of meaning. They talk of reading as a "meaning-making transaction" but then denigrate the idea of "getting the meaning" from the text. There is no "correct" meaning, they say, only plausible meanings. Why is a plausible meaning better than the meaning intended by the author? If there is an accurate way of deriving the meaning the author is tying to convey, why is that not better than a "meaning-making transaction"?

Obviously, whole-language advocates not only have a new definition of reading, but a whole new vocabulary to camouflage the essential idiocy of their philosophy. These same professors write (p. 32):

> Whole language represents a major shift in thinking about the reading process. Rather than viewing reading as "getting the words," whole language educators view reading as essentially a process of creating meanings. (See the development of this view in the writings of Kenneth Goodman [Gollasch 1982] and Frank Smith [1971, 1986].) Meaning is creating through a *transaction* with whole, meaningful texts (i.e. texts, of any length that were written with the intent to communicate meaning). It is a transaction, not an extraction of the meaning *from* the print, in the sense that the *reader-created* meanings are a fusion of what the reader brings and what the text offers.... In a transactional model, words do not have static meanings. Rather they have meaning *potentials* and the capacity to communicate multiple meanings.

This is pretty heady stuff. Note that reading is a transaction with "meaningful texts." A meaningful text is obviously a text pregnant with meaning. But the whole-language reader doesn't extract that meaning. What he or she does is impose a "reader-created" meaning on the text. Does one need a text at all to do that kind of reading? Are they not confusing reading and writing? Writers create meaning when they write something. Readers are supposed to find out what the writer is saying.

Or is it that the whole-language people are not really talking about creating meaning but destroying it? Of course, I am not supposed to extract meaning from what they write. I'm supposed to engage in a transaction and create meaning. But if I did that I'd be accused of misquoting them. You can see how nonsensical their ideas are, because they know the importance of accuracy in what they read and write. After all, they wrote a book, which was copyedited thoroughly by the publisher to make sure that the grammar, spelling, and punctuation were correct. What's the purpose of copyediting if accuracy is not the name of the game? Why is accuracy important for the writer but not for the reader? As writers, these professors of education took great pains to choose the right words in making their case for whole language. And they expect people like me to accurately read what they have written. And as authors, they read their own publishing contracts and the terms of their royalty payments with great accuracy. Or at least their lawyers and agents did. Accuracy is the name of the game in the working world. Or maybe whole language doesn't apply to contracts, insurance policies, and income tax returns.

Can you develop vocabulary without a sense of accuracy? Obviously not, for accuracy is what vocabulary is all about. Some of the statements made by whole-language advocates are so ridiculous as to question the basic brainpower of those who make them. Take, for example, a statement made by James Moffett in his book *Storm in the Mountain: A Case Study of Censorship, Conflict, and Consciousness,* a book about the conflict between parents and teachers over curriculum and textbooks in Kanawha County, West Virginia, in 1974. Moffett writes:

> "God believes in the beauty of phonics" means that those who see themselves as God's spokespeople prefer phonics, precisely, I think, because it shuts out content by focusing the child on particles of language too small to have any meaning. In other words, what phonics really amounts to for those who are sure they have a corner on God's mind but are very unsure of being able to hold their children's minds is *another way to censor books* (unconsciously of course) *by nipping literacy itself in the bud.*

If you're having difficulty grasping the logic of what Mr. Moffett is saying, I don't blame you, because he makes no sense at all. He says that Christians teach their children to read by phonics in order to "nip literacy in the bud," even though this will eventually permit them to read the King James Version of the Bible. Somehow, he assumes that children will be reading "particles of speech" for the rest of their lives and this will "shut out content." Poor Mr. Moffett. Somebody ought to tell this idiot that children are taught intensive phonics in the first grade so that they will be able to become independent readers capable of reading anything they can get their hands on, including, Heaven forbid, Mr. Moffett's strange little book.

Of course, there are whole-language teachers who insist that they do teach phonics — but only in the context of whole-language. That is, they teach graphophonemic cues as one of the strategies in figuring out what the words on the page say. And the graphophonemic cues are only to be used if the picture cues, configuration cues, context cues, syntactic cues, and guessing fail to get the word. That view was very well explained by a whole-language teacher by the name of Martha Bergstresser Ramos who is a reading specialist at the John Glenn Elementary School in San Antonio, Texas. In an article entitled "Sounding off on 'sound it out,'" published in the August/September 1993 issue of *Reading Today*, she writes:

> Reading anthologies nowadays reflect current reading research and have teacher instructions that include encouraging students to integrate picture, context, and graphophonemic cues. It seems apparent that for at least twenty years the words "sound it out" have not been presented as a technique for teachers to learn and use — yet the phrase lives on.
>
> Last year I had an enlightening experience with a first-grade Reading Recovery student. For weeks I had been modeling word identification strategies. I asked him, "Did you get your mouth ready and think what would make sense? Have you checked the picture? Did you check to see if it looks right? What

> do you see about this word that you already know?" And yet, when I asked him, "What can *you* do to figure out the word?" he always answered, "Sound it out!"
>
> One day, in desperation, I asked him, "Who *tells* you to sound it out?"
>
> "My dad," he said.
>
> I should have known. We are not our students' first or only teachers, and this is one reason that the phrase lives on from generation to generation.
>
> [W]e must enlist parents as our teaching allies. We do not want the techniques parents use to help their children read conflict with the reading strategies we are teaching at school. To ensure that parents are helping rather than hindering may require extra parent meetings, seminars, training sessions, and informational bulletins sent home…
>
> We may never be able to discover when people started saying "Sound it out." Some teachers may even choose to continue asking children to sound things out.
>
> I believe, however, that this phrase has outlived its usefulness, and perhaps we should all begin to say "*Think* it out" instead. Then we must give children all the strategies and tools they need for applying their thinking skills to the task of reading.

Ms. Ramos just about sums up everything that is wrong with whole language. In the first place, she does not understand the difference between an alphabetic and an ideographic writing system. Ours is an alphabetic system, which means we use graphic symbols, or letters, that stand for sounds, and the way to become proficient at reading alphabetic writing is to develop a phonetic reflex in which the reader automatically associates letters with sounds. The beauty of developing a phonetic reflex is that with it you can read without having to think it out. You can apply thinking to comprehension rather than to figuring out what the words say in the first place.

In whole language, children are taught to develop a holistic reflex, that is, an automatic way of looking at printed words as whole configurations. A child with a holistic reflex will develop a block against seeing words phonetically. And that's what causes dyslexia. A child who thinks it out instead of sounding it out will be a crippled reader for the rest of his or her life.

A researcher that I work with in North Carolina, Edward Miller, has developed a simple test demonstrating the difference between holistic readers and phonetic readers. He has found that phonetic readers can read anything, but that holistic readers are severely restricted to those words learned by sight or guessed in context. A phonetic reader can easily enlarge his or her vocabulary by sounding out new multisyllabic words encountered in books. But the holistic reader will be severely handicapped by the way he or she looks at words and tries to make heads or tails of them. In fact, according to Miller, all holistic readers are handicapped to some degree, some more severely than others.

Obviously there is more to this whole language business than meets the eye. In fact, there is a political agenda behind whole language which seems to be the driving force behind this movement.

Henry A. Giroux, well-known radical educator who is also director of the Center for Education and Cultural Studies at Miami University (Ohio), writes in *The Whole Language Catalog* (p. 417):

> One of the most important projects for teachers in the next decade will be the development of a critical literacy that incorporates the politics of cultural diversity with a view of pedagogy that recognizes the importance of democratic public life.... Eurocentric culturally dominated curricula must be rejected as resistant to seeing schools as places for educating students to be critical citizens in a vital, democratic society. On the other hand, progressive views of literacy must openly acknowledge their own politics and commitment to pedagogical practices that deepen the goals of democratic struggle and cultural justice.
>
> Whole language has done much to provide educators with both a language of critique and possibility, particularly in terms of its emphasis on the necessity for teachers to incorporate into their teaching the voices that students bring with them to the classroom.

So whole language is more than just another reading program. It is part of the radical leftist program to move America away from its traditional roots — identified by Giroux as our "Eurocentric culturally dominated curricula" — to "democracy," which is simply a code word for socialism. When writing for the general public, socialist educators rarely use the word socialism because they know that it turns people off. So they use the word "democracy" because everybody is supposed to be in favor of it. Nor do they call themselves socialists. They call themselves progressives. And doesn't everyone favor progress?

So we have this semantic deception going on at all times, throwing sand in the eyes of the public, creating verbal confusion, and parental paralysis. It takes something visible like the distribution of condoms to students to wake up parents. It's much easier to recognize a condom than it is to define whole language.

Michael Apple, professor of Curriculum and Instruction and Educational Policy Studies at the University of Wisconsin, Madison, is another leftist concerned about the future of whole language. He is concerned about attacks on public education coming from people like me. He writes (p. 416):

> Conservative groups have nearly always attempted to control the daily lives of teachers and to blame them for serious problems in the larger society over which teachers have little control.... And there are reasons for the current emphasis on an educationally and politically problematic return to a curriculum based on the "western tradition" and "cultural literacy."
>
> This means that — for all its meritorious goals — the whole language movement cannot insure that its own goals and methods will have a lasting and widespread impact unless it is willing to act not only

> within the school, but outside it as well. Its proponents need to join with others in the wider social movements that aim at democratizing our economy, politics, and culture, and that act against a society that is so unequal in gender, race, and class terms.

Obviously Mr. Apple identifies the whole language movement as being part of the radical leftist movement to "democratize" — meaning socialize — our society. That whole language is part of the political agenda of the left was confirmed by two of the authors of *Whole Language; What's the Difference?*, Bess Altwerger and Barbara Flores. In an article entitled "The Politics of Whole Language" published in *The Whole Language Catalog* (p. 418), they write:

> Whole language teaching is subversive, in the best sense of the word, because it seeks to restore equality and democracy to our schools, to our children, and in essence, to our society.
>
> Whole language puts power for learning, decision-making, and problem-solving back into the hands of teachers and students. It creates active learners; it empowers all of us to act upon and transform our environments and society in general. We are not just asking for a change in the teaching of reading, but a radical change in the social and political structure of schooling and society.

There you have it, as clearly and unequivocally stated, that there is a political agenda behind whole language. Also, as many of you know, whole language is considered to be part of the holistic education movement. Don Miller, founder and editor of

Holistic Education Review defines holistic education as follows (p. 427):

> Holistic education seeks to nurture the development of the whole person. It is not enough to educate for academic achievement and vocational skills alone; the human personality is an integrated complex of intellectual, physical, social, moral, emotional, and spiritual possibilities. All of these must be taken into account in the education of children....
>
> Holistic education is a spiritual worldview rather than a materialist one. It is belief in, and a reverence for, a self-directed life force that lies beyond our rational, intellectual understanding.

Miller goes on to say that holistic spirituality is not religion, but "self-actualization," the process outlined by humanist psychologist Abraham Maslow. What is quite clear, however, is that holistic education gets into areas that public schools have no business getting into: the spiritual and emotional lives of its students. Miller continues:

> The holistic perspective is an inclusive, phenomenological, ecological, global perspective that seeks to encompass all aspects of human experience.... [H]olistic education is a radical break from traditional ways of understanding human development.... [I]t represents a new paradigm. In essence, it is the educational approach of a new culture — an emerging postindustrial, post-technocratic civilization, in which the whole human being may yet be nurtured.

And you thought kids go to school just to learn to read and write!

Perhaps what makes whole language so appealing to so many teachers is that it deals with the whole child, it nurtures, it cuddles. There is no ability grouping, older kids help younger kids, and the kids are active learners reading real books not textbooks. There's lots of dialogue, lots of "critical thinking." It's as if the classroom were transformed into a surrogate home, replacing the child's real home by offering so much more "enrichment" and bonding than parents can provide. A perfect scheme for weaning children away from their traditional religious upbringing and inculcating them in the liberating, empowering dogma of holistic, ecological paganism.

There's another aspect of whole language of which you should be aware. It is called *deconstruction*. *The Academic American Encyclopedia* defines deconstruction as follows (Volume. 6, p. 76):

> Deconstructionism is a theory about language and literature that developed in the 1970s.... Its initial premises were first formulated by the French philosopher and critic Jacques Derrida, whose works converted a number of U.S. academics....
>
> What most characterizes deconstruction is its notion of textuality, a view of language as it exists not only in books, but in speech, in history and in culture. For the deconstructionist, language constitutes everything. The world itself is "text." Language shapes humanity and creates human reality.... Yet, upon close

> examination, words seem to have no necessary connection with reality or with concepts or ideas.

Note the strange contradiction: language creates human reality, but words have no necessary connection with reality. Whole-language educators promote the same sort of contradiction. Children are expected to "read for meaning," but are encouraged to invent meaning. After all, when they speak of "reader-created meanings," what limits do they place on the reader's creativity? The article continues:

> Given the numerous hidden links of a text to its cultural and social intertext, the text's content and meaning are, essentially indeterminate. Texts, therefore, are unreadable, and the practice of interpretation may be defined as *misreading*.
>
> [Derrida attacks] what he calls "logocentrism," the human habit of assigning truth to *logos* — to spoken language, the voice of reason, the word of God. Derrida finds that logocentrism generates and depends upon a framework of two-term oppositions that are basic to Western thinking, such as being/non-being, thing/word, truth/lie. male/female. In the logocentric epistemological system the first term of each pair is privileged (TRUTH/lie, MALE, female). Derrida is critical of these hierarchical polarities, and seeks to take tradition apart by reversing their order and displacing, and thus transforming, each of the terms.

Thus, deconstruction is basically an attack on the notion of absolute truth and literal comprehension of a written text. Western thinking, linear thinking, is "logocentric" in that it relies on the word as the means of conveying truth. Critics of traditional teaching methods are keenly aware of the difference between the logocentric approach and the whole-language approach. In an article entitled, "Political Philosophy and Reading Make a Dangerous Mix," published in *Education Week,* February 27, 1985, the authors wrote:

> After spending six years observing the efforts of the self-styled "New Right" to influence education throughout the country, we have found a pattern of activities that could, if some members of the New Right are successful, cause a very limited model for teaching reading to prevail in both public and private schools. The model is based on the belief that literal comprehension is the only goal of reading instruction. Because it trains children to reason in a very limited manner, it is a model that we believe could have serious political consequences in a country where the ability of the citizenry to read and think critically is an essential determinant of democratic governance....
>
> By attempting to control the kinds of materials and questions teachers and students may use; by limiting reading instruction to systematic phonics instruction, sound-symbol decoding, and literal comprehension and by aiming its criticism at reading books story lines in an effort to influence content, the New Right's philosophy runs counter to the research findings and theoretical perspectives of most noted reading authorities.

Have you ever heard anything quite as ridiculous as this coming out of the mouths of educators? They're telling us that the way George Washington,

Thomas Jefferson, and Abraham Lincoln were taught to read is going to adversely affect democratic governance. This "very limited model for teaching reading" produced that remarkable group of intellects known as our Founding Fathers who proceeded to create the greatest, freest, and richest nation on earth. I prefer their governance to anything the educators have in mind.

Finally an article about Derrida in *Contemporary Authors* (Volume 124, p. 112) states:

> [D]econstructionism emphasizes the reader's role in extracting meaning from texts and the impossibility of determining absolute meaning.

Which is what whole language teaches. When all is said and done, the aim of the whole-language movement is simply to destroy the literary underpinnings of our Judeo-Christian civilization: individualism, capitalism, and the idea of absolute truth. Individualism is undermined by the emphasis on group work, cooperative learning, and peer dependency; capitalism is undermined by emphasizing collectivist activities; and religion is undermined by attacking the word, *logos*, the Word of God as absolute truth.

Does the dumbing down process have anything to do with this idea of a New World Order? I'm afraid it does. What are the goals of this new system of world governance? In essence, it is to create a socially controlled, pagan world government, organized as a three-tier pyramidal society. In this setup, the elite rule at the top, and directly beneath them are the favored professionals, scientists, artists, and corporate heads who keep the economy going. Directly beneath them are the rest of us, suitably dumbed down and conditioned to do the bidding of the elite and managerial overseers without complaint.

Dumbing down the masses is a very important part of the scheme, and whole language is calculated to do just that, to turn most people into functional literates — that is, to be able to read at a very low level, so that they will be completely dependent on TV for guidance and enlightenment. To prove this, let me quote a member of the elite by the name of Professor Anthony Oettinger of Harvard University who also happens to be a member of the Council on Foreign Relations. This is what he told an audience of corporate executives in 1981 (*The Innisbrook Papers*, February 1982, pp. 19-21, edited proceedings of a Northern Telecom senior management conference):

> Our idea of literacy I am afraid, is obsolete because it rests on a frozen and classical definition.... The present "traditional" concept of literacy has to do with the ability to read and write. But the real question that confronts us today is: How do we help citizens function well in their society? How can they acquire the skills necessary to solve their problems?
>
> Do we, for example, really want to teach people to do a lot of sums or write in "a fine round hand" when they have a five-dollar hand-held calculator or a word processor to work with? Or, do we really have to have everybody literate...writing and reading in the traditional sense...when we have the means

> through our technology to achieve a new flowering of oral communication?
>
> It is the traditional idea that says certain forms of communication, such as comic books, are "bad." But in the modern context of functionalism they may not be all that bad.
>
> We have the potential for using the cathode ray tube to transmit pictorial information and for developing it to a much greater extent than we have as a dynamic form of communication, whose implications for training and schooling and so on are quite different from linear print or "frozen" literacy.

There you have it. The voice of the elite who think that comic-book literacy is good enough for the masses. Training and schooling is to be changed from reliance on linear print and "frozen" literacy to a dependence on TV pictorial information. Now, I don't know any parents who send their children to school to learn to read comic books or believe that traditional literacy is obsolete. But apparently Professor Oettinger and his colleagues have more say over how children are to be taught than their parents.

Another member of the elite who has some interesting things to say about literacy is an adult literacy expert by the name of Thomas Sticht who once worked for our Secretary of Labor Robert Reich. Mr. Sticht was reported in *The Washington Post* (8/17/87) as saying:

> Many companies have moved operations to places with cheap, relatively poorly educated labor. What may be crucial, they say is the dependability of a labor force and how well it can be managed and

> trained...not its general educational level, although a small cadre of highly educated creative people is essential to innovation and growth. Ending discrimination and changing values are probably more important than reading in moving low-income families into the middle class.

In other words, don't bother to teach American kids American history or English literature or Latin or about the Declaration of Independence and the Constitution. After all, Taiwanese and Mexican workers have not been taught these subjects and they make efficient workers. And that's what the multinational corporations need.

Whole language and Outcome Based Education will give the elite exactly what it wants: a dumbed down, docile population that can be trained and managed by the elite to serve the elite.

Thomas Jefferson advocated universal free education as a means of preserving our free republic. But the present American elite is perverting that system in order to destroy this free republic, or what's left of it. But as long as we can meet here and I can speak my mind, the war is by no means over. There will be many more battles in the days ahead and we must fight until we return America to what it once was, the fulfillment of a Biblical vision of a righteous society whose laws conform to the Ten Commandments. That's what our Founding Fathers gave us, and nobody called it a theocracy. They called it a Republic.

Index of Contents

A

B

C

D

E

F

G

H

I

J

K

L

M

N

O

P

R

S

T

U

V

W

Y

Samuel L. Blumenfeld is the author of eight books on education:

Born and educated in New York City, Mr. Blumenfeld graduated from the City College of New York in 1950, studied in France for two years, then worked for ten years as an editor in the New York book publishing industry. In 1970 he began writing full time. His book, **Is Public Education Necessary?**, has been described by one reviewer as one of the most important books about education ever written. Peter Brimelow in *Fortune* called it "brilliant revisionist history."

Mr. Blumenfeld's writings have appeared in such diverse publications as *Reason, Inquiry, The Chalcedon Report, Insight, Education Digest, Vital Speeches, American Education, Boston Magazine, American Legion Magazine, The Teaching Home, Practical Homeschooling, Home School Digest, The Whistleblower,* and on such Internet sites as World Net Daily, Enter Stage Right, Opinion Net, and others. He has taught in both public and private schools, including one for children with learning and behavioral problems.

Mr. Blumenfeld has spoken at educational conferences sponsored by The Heritage Foundation, Reading Reform Foundation, Thomas Alva Edison Foundation, American Legislative Exchange Council, Concerned Women for America, Eagle Forum, Hillsdale College, Bob Jones University, Pensacola Christian College, Chalcedon Foundation, Separation of School and State Alliance, the Constitutional Coalition, and many homeschool conventions. He has lectured widely in the U.S., Canada, Australia and New Zealand and has been a frequent guest on radio and TV talk shows.

In 1986, Mr. Blumenfeld was awarded an Honorary Doctor of Laws degree by Bob Jones University. He also served in the U.S. Army in World War II and took part in combat during the last weeks of the Italian campaign.